The MAILBOX®

The Education Center®

Language Arts
Choose & Do Grids

grades 4-6

Over 375 Differentiated Activities

**42 grids!
42 practice pages!**

- Reading comprehension
- Literary response
- Word analysis, fluency, and vocabulary
- Writing conventions
- Writing applications
- Reference skills
- Spelling

Skill practice that gives students choices!

D1287582

Managing Editor: Becky S. Andrews

Editorial Team: Debbie Ashworth, Diane Badden, Kimberley Bruck, Karen A. Brudnak, Pam Crane, Chris Curry, David Drews, Tazmen Hansen, Marsha Heim, Lori Z. Henry, Troy Lawrence, Kitty Lowrance, Teri Nielsen, Mark Rainey, Greg D. Rieves, Hope Rodgers-Medina, Rebecca Saunders, Karen P. Shelton, Donna K. Teal, Patricia Twohey, Sharon M. Tresino, Zane Williard

www.themailbox.com

©2012 The Mailbox® Books
All rights reserved.
ISBN 978-1-61276-210-4

Printed in the United States
10 9 8 7 6 5 4 3 2 1
HPS233483

What's

42 Activity Grids
Nine choices on every grid!

═══ Simple and Compound Sentences ═══

Name _____

Date _____

Choose ____ or more activities to do.
When you finish an activity, color its number.

1 Unscramble each simple sentence and write it correctly. Underline the complete subject once and the complete predicate twice. • predicate and a sentence a a subject has simple • sentences two at sentence a compound contains least simple	**2** Read one or more sports articles. Copy three simple and three compound sentences. Underline the complete subjects once and the complete predicates twice. 	**3** Change each compound sentence into two simple sentences. Underline the complete subjects once and the complete predicates twice. • The Statue of Liberty holds a torch in her right hand, and she grasps a tablet in her left hand. • The Liberty Bell was rung at the first public reading of the Declaration of Independence, but it cracked badly on Washington's Birthday in 1846.
4 Change each simple sentence into a compound sentence. • A hurricane is forecasted. • An unusually late frost damaged crops. • The area had experienced drought.	**5** Do the practice page "Storm Watch."	**6** Label cards with the words below. Shuffle the cards and stack them facedown. Draw a card. Use the word to make a simple sentence and then a compound one. Repeat three more times. precipitation, fog, cloudy, frost, showers, rain, wind, temperature, morning
7 Write three simple and three compound sentences about your favorite school subject. Simple Sentence <u>Our music teacher</u> <u>shows us how to play rhythms.</u> Compound Sentence <u>We make the beat with our bodies</u>, and <u>we take turns playing the drums.</u>	**8** Write four compound sentences about the selections you would order at your favorite restaurant. I want to order a milk shake, but I can't drink it all. I'll have a foot-long hot dog, and fries sound good too.	**9** Write four compound sentences about dogs on paper strips, leaving spaces for conjunctions. Attach conjunctions written on bone cutouts. Labs are popular pets, {but} they can be terrible chewers. Collies are herding dogs, {and} they tend to bark a lot. 

Choose & Do Language Arts Grids • ©The Mailbox® Books • TEC61227 • Key p. 94

Note to the teacher: Provide sports articles for activity 2. Program the student directions with the number of activities to be completed. Then copy the page and page 54 (back-to-back if desired) for each student.

53

Inside

42 Practice Pages
Always activity 5 on the grid

Simple and Compound Sentences

Name _____ Date _____

Storm Watch

Use the key to label each sentence.

Key
S = simple sentence
C = compound sentence

_____ 1. Air is blowing, sinking, and rising all the time.

_____ 2. Hurricanes form over the ocean.

_____ 3. Meteorologists track storms, and they use computers to track the paths storms take.

_____ 4. Special planes are flown into storms to get information.

_____ 5. The National Weather Service tells us what to expect.

_____ 6. Broadcasts inform us of the forecast, but it's up to us to take precautions.

_____ 7. A warning means a hurricane is likley to reach land, and your next step should be to get to a safe place.

_____ 8. Bring in things like toys, flowerpots, and folding chairs.

_____ 9. Wind could pick up objects in your yard, and it could toss them toward your windows.

_____ 10. During a storm, stay inside where it is safe.

_____ 11. Storms can produce hail, and large hail can do a lot of damage.

_____ 12. Thunderstorms can happen in winter, but they are more common in warm weather.

_____ 13. Storms sometimes bring heavy rains, and the rains can cause dangerous floods.

_____ 14. Lightning strikes the tallest objects, so get down low if you're outside.

_____ 15. People are sometimes struck by lightning, but most of them survive it.

Change two of the simple sentences above into compound sentences.

• _____

_____

• _____

Choose & Do Language Arts Grids • ©The Mailbox® Books

Tip!
To save paper, copy a grid and its practice page back-to-back!

Independent practice for
- **Morning work**
- **Center work**
- **Homework**
- **Free time**
- **Anytime**

Answer keys on pages 90-96.

Table of Contents

Spelling

Reading Comprehension

Literary Response

Word Analysis, Fluency, and Vocabulary

Writing Conventions

Writing Applications

Reference Skills

Easily Confused Words

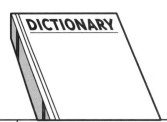

Name _____

Date _____

Choose ____ or more activities to do.
When you finish an activity, color its number.

1 Use *it's* or *its* to write a sentence with each of the following phrases. _____ a bouncing baby boy. _____ about time. _____ buttons were gone. _____ now or never. 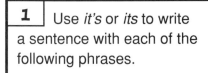 it + is = **it's**	**2** Write the headings "breath" and "breathe." Sort the phrases and complete each one. mumble under your _____ _____ of fresh air _____ new life into _____ deeply catch your _____	**3** Both of these words have a short *e* sound: *lead* and *led*. Write four sentences for each. Use a dictionary to guide you. DICTIONARY
4 Write the headings "lose" and "loose." Sort the phrases and complete each one. a _____ tooth wear your hair _____ nothing to _____ _____ sleep a _____ plank _____ his way	**5** Do the practice page "School Daze Days." 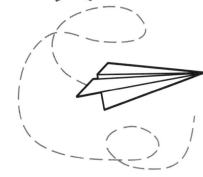	**6** Design a mini poster called "What a difference a vowel makes!" On it, compare the meanings of the words below that sound alike. Add illustrations. **stationary** **stationery** **principal** **principle** **dual** **duel**
7 Draw a grid and label it. Beneath each word, write its definition. Then write three sentences correctly using each word. | cite	site	sight | |===|===|===| 1. 1. 1. 2. 2. 2. 3. 3. 3.	**8** Fold a sheet of paper in half. Label it as shown. Write three sentences using each word. accept — to receive / except — to take out 1. 1. 2. 2. 3. 3.	**9** Cut out a symmetrical shape. Write a confusing word pair on it. Include a definition and a sentence for each word. **affect** verb to influence A good coach can affect his players' skills. **effect** noun result The rain had a disastrous effect.

Choose & Do Language Arts Grids • ©The Mailbox® Books • TEC61227 • Key p. 90

Note to the teacher: Provide small pieces of poster board for activity 6 and colorful paper and markers for activity 9. Program the student directions with the number of activities to be completed. Then copy the page and page 6 (back-to-back if desired) for each student.

Easily Confused Words

Name _____ Date _____

School ~~Daze~~ Days

Choose the correct word to complete each sentence.
Use a dictionary.

loose	its	
breath	effect	
lead	cite	
it's	lose	
personnel	breathe	
except	led	
personal	dual	
duel	site	
accept	affect	

1. _____ almost time for our science exam.

2. The projector just blew _____ bulb.

3. No homework? Don't hold your _____.

4. When he sees this grade, he will _____ a sigh of relief.

5. The pencil _____ always breaks!

6. Several factors _____ to his suspension.

7. If you _____ your study guide, you will regret it.

8. The leg of my desk wiggles because it's _____.

9. Because it contains _____ information, the envelope is sealed.

10. School _____ frown upon chewing gum at school.

11. The two runners were in a _____ for first place.

12. There are _____ methods for contacting the principal.

13. When you write a report, you must _____ your sources.

14. The _____ for our school garden has been staked off.

15. Everyone _____ Trevor has returned his form on time.

16. She will _____ my excuse about what happened.

17. Weather can really _____ my mood.

18. Today's sunshine had a good _____ on my mood.

Inflected Endings: -ed, -ing

Name _____

Date _____

Choose ___ or more activities to do.
When you finish an activity, color its number.

---

1 Rewrite the words below, adding -ed and -ing. These words drop their silent e's before the endings.

brave	spike	pave
zone	mute	time
save	smile	quake

---

2 Some endings indicate tense. Scan through a book. Locate and write ten words with each ending below.

present tense -ing	past tense -ed
biking	walked
skipping	camped
cooking	hopped

---

3 Label a card as shown. Find ten verbs that fit the description. Write each word and its inflected forms on the card.

> If the ending y follows a vowel, just add -ed or -ing.

Example:
replay   replayed   replaying

---

4 Label a card as shown. Find ten verbs that fit the description. Write each word and its inflected forms on the card.

> If the ending y follows a consonant, change the y to i and add -ed. Keep the y when adding -ing.

Example:
replied   replying

---

5 Do the practice page "The Munching Mantis."

---

6 Label a card as shown. Find ten verbs that fit the description. Write each word and its inflected form on the card.

> a vowel followed by one consonant

EXAMPLE: KNIT KNITTING
DOUBLE THE FINAL CONSONANT BEFORE ADDING -ING.

---

7 Label a card as shown. Find ten verbs that fit the description. Write each word and its inflected form on the card.

> vowel-vowel-consonant words

Example: scream screaming
Do nothing before adding -ing.

---

8 Write a letter mentioning things you have done in the past and things you are currently doing. Use at least four -ing and four -ed words.

---

9 Rewrite this paragraph, correcting the spelling errors. Underline each word you fix.

I carryed my cell phone as I walkeed to your house. Joe phoneed and askt if I was planing on staing and playng with you. I inviteed him to join us. He is racing here now. I tryed to call you, but your phone was busy.

Choose & Do Language Arts Grids • ©The Mailbox® Books • TEC61227 • Key p. 90

Note to the teacher: Supply an assortment of texts and large index cards or half sheets of paper for activities 2–4, 6, and 7. Program the student directions with the number of activities to be completed. Then copy the page and page 8 (back-to-back if desired) for each student.

7

Name _____ Date _____

The Munching Mantis

Fill each blank with an *-ed* or *-ing* form of a word from the word bank.
Cross out each word as you use it.

_____ mantises are found in the United States. They can also be

_____ in tropical places around the world. _____ one

is not easy. Mantises are very good at _____ in with the plants they are

_____ on. Mantises come in all sizes, _____ from one

centimeter long to six inches long.

 Mantises are known for _____ with their arms _____

up. This pose makes them look as though they are praying. Motionless, they seem to be

_____ the area with their huge eyes. These eyes are _____

on a triangular head. This head turns 180 degrees for _____ prey. When an

insect comes within _____ distance, the mantis snatches it with its

_____ forelegs. Then the praying mantis uses its mouth parts to start

_____ and _____ through the insect's body.

 Sometimes, however, this predator can become prey. Male praying mantises fly at night.

They are _____ to lights. Bats use sound waves that help in

_____ insects like mantises. A praying mantis only has one ear. It uses its ear

as a tool for _____ and _____ a bat attack. If a

_____ mantis senses a mild threat from a bat, it begins slowly

_____. But if it senses a deadly threat, it begins _____

and _____ toward the ground, _____ itself from the

clutches of the bat.

Word Bank for *-ing* endings

cut	detect	dodge	fly	save
pray	hear	blend	scan	dive
locate	spot	twirl	range	rest
pose	tear	strike	turn	

Word Bank for *-ed* endings.

attract	prop	mount
spike	locate	

Spelling

Name _____

Date _____

Choose ___ or more activities to do.
When you finish an activity, color its number.

1 Find two synonyms each for half of your spelling words. Use a thesaurus. List each word and its synonyms. **hungry** **empty** **starved**	**2** Choose three words. Write and illustrate an acrostic poem about each word. **W**onder spun of silken threads **E**ver so carefully sewn **B**eaded now with drops of dew	**3** Write each of your words using the following color code. prefix = green root = red suffix = blue none of the above = orange
4 Choose six words. Compose a sentence to help you remember its spelling. **propel** **P**lump **r**abbits **o**bserved **p**eople **e**ating **l**ettuce.	**5** Do the practice page "Coordinate Spelling."	**6** Find a word in a dictionary. Flag and read the entries. Share four of your most interesting findings with a friend.
7 Write each word on a paper slip. Sort to classify the words in each of the following ways: • **by part of speech** • **by number of letters** • **by number of syllables** • **by initial consonant or vowel** • **in alphabetical order**	**8** Use graph paper to make a word search puzzle of your words. Have a friend complete the puzzle. 	**9** Write lost-and-found ads for four words. Describe each word clearly without naming it. Ask a friend to read the ads and guess your words. This well-rounded, two-syllable word begins like *credit* and *crest*. The second syllable is another word for a *penny*. If seen, call 555-0001. Answer: crescent

---

Note to the teacher: Provide sticky notes for activity 6, slips of paper for activity 7, and graph paper for activity 8. Program the student directions with the number of activities to be completed. Then copy the page and page 10 (back-to-back if desired) for each student.

Name _____   Date _____

Coordinate Spelling

Choose 12 words from your spelling list.
Write the coordinate pairs to spell each word.
Ask a friend to decode each word.

Use with your own word list!

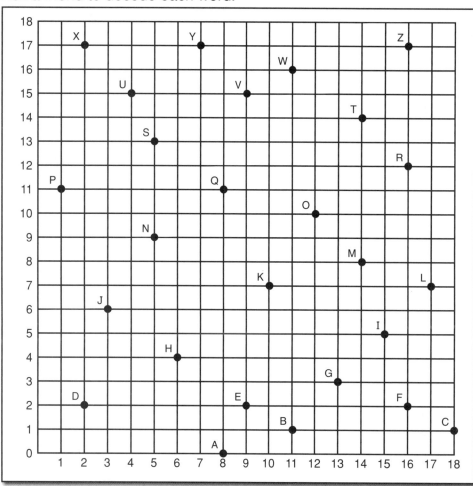

Example: (9,2), (5,9), (8,0), (11,1), (17,7), (9,2) = *enable*

1. _____   7. _____

2. _____   8. _____

3. _____   9. _____

4. _____   10. _____

5. _____   11. _____

6. _____   12. _____

Spelling

Name _____

Date _____

Choose ___ or more activities to do.
When you finish an activity, color its number.

---

1 Find two antonyms each for five of your spelling words. List each word and its antonyms.

My Word	Antonym	Antonym
ordinary	abnormal	unusual

---

2 Choose the most interesting word on your list. Cut out related words and pictures from old magazines to make a mini collage.

---

3 Write your words using the code below and colored pencils.

root, base, or familiar part = red
prefix = blue
suffix = green
inflected ending (-ed, -ing) = orange
plural ending = purple
none of the above = brown

---

4 Choose five of the most challenging words on your list. Complete a word map for each word.

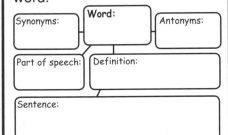

Synonyms: | Word: | Antonyms:
Part of speech: | Definition:
Sentence:

---

5 Do the practice page "Splashy Spelling Adventures."

---

6 Select six words. In an envelope, place clues related to those words. Have a pal look at each clue, guess the word, and spell it.

Example: disease

FLU SHOTS
No appointment necessary.

---

7 Create riddles for half of your spelling words. Post them where others will read them.

I'm a six-letter word that's a synonym of *messy.*
I have the prefix *un-.*
What word am I?

Answer: untidy

---

8 On graph paper, make a crossword puzzle with at least half of your words. Trade your puzzle with someone else who made one. Complete your pal's puzzle.

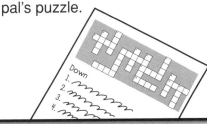

---

9 Design a cartoon strip. Include at least eight of your words in the characters' dialogue.

A Pumpkin Head's Life

Choose & Do Language Arts Grids • ©The Mailbox® Books • TEC61227

Note to the teacher: Provide old magazines and small pieces of construction paper for activity 2, envelopes for activity 6, and graph paper for activity 8. Program the student directions with the number of activities to be completed. Then copy the page and page 12 (back-to-back if desired) for each student.

Name _____

Date _____

Spelling

Splashy Spelling Adventures

Copy each of your spelling words wherever it fits the description.
Underline the part or parts that qualify it for that location.

two syllables

three or more syllables

prefix

suffix

short-vowel sound

r-controlled vowel

long-vowel sound

silent letter

Choose & Do Language Arts Grids • ©The Mailbox® Books • TEC61227

Note to the teacher: Use with page 11.

Main Idea and Supporting Details

Name _____

Date _____

Choose ___ or more activities to do.
When you finish an activity, color its number.

1 Read a newspaper article. Change the headline into a main idea sentence. Then write four supporting details. **City Times**	**2** Write four great things about your favorite sport. Then write a related main idea. Draft a paragraph convincing others that your favorite sport is wonderful.	**3** Draw a larger version of this organizer. Read some informational text and complete the organizer. Topic: Main idea: Detail: Detail: Detail:
4 As you read a section from a science book, write the main idea for each paragraph. Then use these notes to write the main idea for the section.	**5** Do the practice page "A Recipe for Understanding."	**6** Read a poem. Write its main idea. Then copy three pieces of evidence from the poem that support the main idea. Share your work with a friend. *Poetry*
7 Write the main idea of a product advertisement. Write to explain how you know. **What does the ad show?** **What does the ad say?** **Remove-o** **Gets stains out!**	**8** List four things that are annoying about a certain animal. Write a main idea that goes with those things. Write a paragraph using these thoughts. **Grrrr...**	**9** Read a comic strip. Write its main idea. Then write at least three things from the strip that prove you've identified the main point. • **something said** • **expressions shown** • **character's actions** **Funny Paper**

Choose & Do Language Arts Grids • ©The Mailbox® Books • TEC61227

Note to the teacher: Supply newspapers for activity 1, print advertisements for activity 7, and comic strips for activity 9. Program the student directions with the number of activities to be completed. Then copy the page and page 14 (back-to-back if desired) for each student.

Name _____

Date _____

Main Idea and Supporting Details

A Recipe for Understanding

Read each story.
Then complete its boxed section.

A chef wears many different hats. He must put together plans for scrumptious menus. A chef also orders the food and supplies needed to make the plans come to life. Although he might cook some dishes himself, he often teaches other cooks how to prepare foods in tasty ways. Then, as orders come to the kitchen, it's the chef who makes sure all the cooks and kitchen staff carefully prepare the food. If a chef has done all his jobs well, his customers enjoy every yummy bite.

Main idea: _____
_____
_____

Detail 1: _____

Detail 2: _____

Detail 3: _____

Detail 4: _____

Have you ever thought about all the places that chefs work? Of course, some work in restaurants. Some chefs also work in health-care facilities and hospitals where folks need special diets. Other chefs prepare meals at hotels, lodges, or resorts. Some of them are in charge of preparing fancy meals aboard cruise ships. Still others prepare food for large events, such as weddings and parties. Wherever there's a hungry crowd, chances are there's a busy chef nearby.

Main idea: _____
_____

Detail 1: _____

Detail 2: _____

Detail 3: _____

Detail 4: _____

Note to the teacher: Use with page 13.

Cause and Effect

Name _____

Date _____

Choose ___ or more activities to do.
When you finish an activity, color its number.

1 Write the headings shown. Find related word pairs below and write them under the correct headings. Add five more pairs.

dust	tears	alarm
bruise	sneeze	fall
awake	joke	laughter
	grief	

cause	effect

2 Draw and label five arrows and targets as shown. Recall characters' actions from a story you've read. Label the shapes to show causes and effects.

Cause — Jack traded the cow for magic beans.
Effect — His mother was upset about the trade.

3 In a passage, hunt for the words below, which can signal cause-and-effect relationships. List each cause and effect that you find.

because
since
therefore
if, then

4 Read an article about a disaster or problem. On a card, write what it was. On other cards, write the effects of that problem. Clip the cards together.

A tornado devastated a college town.
The National C___
The Red Cross offered food, water, and assistance.

5 Do the practice page "Spider Specialties."

IF you do your best, **then** you'll be very proud.

6 Draw a web for each cause below. Complete each web by labeling several lines with effects that might result from each cause.

- Someone saved a child.
- Someone was kind to a grandmother.
- Someone lied.

Someone lied.

7 Label a sheet of paper as shown. List five causes that can lead to each emotion.

happiness	anger	excitement
sorrow	disappointment	jealousy

8 Read an informational passage. Fold your paper in half and label it with the headings shown. Write five cause-and-effect relationships from the passage.

cause	effect
Fruit growers use pesticides to get rid of insects.	Dangerous chemicals end up in our air and water.

9 Create a timeline of five events that happened yesterday. For each event, write a sentence that explains the cause or effect of the event.

7:30—I almost missed the school bus because I overslept.

Choose & Do Language Arts Grids • ©The Mailbox® Books • TEC61227 • Key p. 90

Note to the teacher: Supply paper clips, hole punchers, and index cards for activity 4. Program the student directions with the number of activities to be completed. Then copy the page and page 16 (back-to-back if desired) for each student.

15

Cause and Effect

Name _____ Date _____

Spider Specialties

Copy the matching cause or effect in each row.

Web phrases:
- Spiderwebs are hard to see.
- This allows them to grow larger.
- Spiders can travel great distances, even out to sea.
- This lets them know it's time to eat.
- Sometimes spiders aren't ready to eat their prey.
- Baby spiders stay inside their egg sacs for a while.
- Spiders eat many, many insects.
- Spiders often need to make quick escapes.
- They don't get stuck in their own webs.
- Spiders make webs with strands of sticky silk.

cause	effect
Baby spiders must be able to spin their own silk.	
Spiderlings shed their exoskeletons and grow new ones.	
	An insect may not see a web and fly right into it.
	A trapped insect only gets more stuck as it struggles.
Spiders can feel trapped insects tugging on their webs.	
Spiders know where the sticky parts of their webs are.	
	They make a silk case around it and put it in a safe place for later.
	Spiders can help farmers get rid of insect pests.
	They descend on silk threads that can be quickly climbed.
Small spiders release silk threads and get carried away on breezes.	

Note to the teacher: Use with page 15.

Facts and Opinions

Name _____

Date _____

Choose ___ or more activities to do.
When you finish an activity, color its number.

1 Look up *fact* and *opinion* in a dictionary. Write each meaning in your own words. Then write four facts and four opinions about yourself. **fact** | **opinion** I am twice as old as my little sister, Allison. | I am the best runner in my family.	**2** Facts often contain names, dates, places, events, and numbers. Read a news article looking for these kinds of clues. Highlight each fact you find. **Record Rain**	**3** Read an article or advertisement. Look for words like those below that can signal opinions. Highlight each opinion you find. think · feel · believe greatest · worst · beautiful terrible · wonderful · good best · more · most important · ugly · better
4 Pretend you are interviewing a famous person. Write six questions you can ask to learn facts about this person. Then write six questions to learn about this person's opinions.	**5** Do the practice page "Is That a Fact?" 	**6** Write a paragraph containing facts about a book you've read. Then write another one filled with your opinions about the book. Facts This book was written in 1989. The author wrote a sequel.
7 Fold your paper in half. Then unfold and label it as shown. Write facts about a topic of your choice on the front strips. Write opinions about the topic on the back strips. 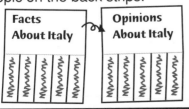	**8** On separate cards, copy five facts from an article. Also write five related opinions. Shuffle. Have a friend sort the facts from the opinions. 	**9** Read a sports article. Design a collector's card about an event or athlete mentioned in the article. Include four facts and four opinions. 

Choose & Do Language Arts Grids • ©The Mailbox® Books • TEC61227

Note to the teacher: Supply newspaper articles for activities 2, 3, and 8 and sports articles for activity 9. Program student directions with the number of activities to be completed. Then copy the page and page 18 (back-to-back if desired) for each student.

Facts and Opinions

Name _____   Date _____

Is That a Fact?

Shade each box that features a fact.
Underline the clue word or words in each opinion.

1. Most pizzerias use more than 50 pizza boxes each day.

2. Americans spend too much of their food budget on pizza.

3. The best pizza on the planet is made in Nome, Alaska.

4. More than one-third of all pizza orders include pepperoni as a topping.

5. More than 90 percent of Americans eat pizza frequently.

6. A good tip for a pizza delivery driver is two dollars.

7. Pizza delivery drivers get larger tips on Super Bowl Sunday.

8. In America, about 350 pizza slices are eaten each second.

9. Hand-tossed crust has better flavor than rolled crust.

10. There are more than 60,000 pizzerias in the United States.

11. It's terrible to put gourmet toppings like caviar on pizza.

12. Each American eats about 46 slices of pizza each year.

13. The worst pizza topping of all time is squid.

14. Each year, about five billion pizzas are sold worldwide.

15. In the United States, 14 inches is the most popular pizza size.

16. Hawaiian pizza, with its golden pineapple chunks, is a wonderful choice.

17. The world's biggest pizza was more than 120 feet in diameter.

18. Fried egg pizzas will never be popular in the United States.

Summarizing

Name _____

Date _____

Choose ___ or more activities to do.
When you finish an activity, color its number.

1 Write a summary of the following text. Make it concise and leave out unimportant details.

A girl practiced piano many hours each day. She took lessons every week. Her whole family came to her piano competition. She was nervous. She wore a red dress. She earned a blue ribbon and was very happy.

2 Complete three webs like those below for a story you recently read. Highlight the things that were most important. Then use your highlights to summarize the story.

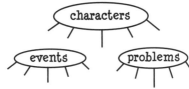

3 List the events in a story you recently read. Cut the events apart and choose the most important ones. Use only those to write a summary.

A bad storm caused a boat to be shipwrecked.

Blaine used parts of the wreck to make a shelter.

The crew signaled for help until the batteries died.

4 Write a summary of a book you've read using less than 30 words. To help write your summary, complete a grid with the headings shown.

somebody	wanted	but	so
three orphaned children	a new mother	they found someone different from their birth mother	they learned to live a new life with a totally different kind of mother

5 Do the practice page "Summing It Up."

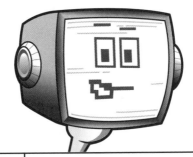

6 Make a poster that explains how retelling and summarizing are different.

Retelling a Story
Is Not
Summarizing a Story

Retelling is...

Summarizing is...

7 On separate cards, write how a story you've read begins and ends. On additional cards, write the other important events. Then write a summary.

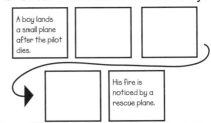

A boy lands a small plane after the pilot dies.

His fire is noticed by a rescue plane.

8 List the big ideas from an informational text. Have a partner time you as you summarize the ideas. Need more than two minutes? Edit your list and try again.

00:45

9 Evaluate one of your summaries using these guidelines. Edit and rewrite if necessary.

Does this summary contain the important big ideas?

Does it contain unimportant or repeated information? If so, remove it.

Does it contain facts or details? If so, remove them.

Note to the teacher: Program student directions with the number of activities to be completed. Then copy the page and page 20 (back-to-back if desired) for each student.

19

Summarizing

Summing It Up

Choose and write the question that each paragraph answers. Then answer each question in your own words to summarize the paragraph.

Questions to choose from:
How does a robot know what to do?
Why are robots needed?
What kinds of jobs can robots do?

WARNING! State only the big ideas.

1 A robot is a machine that works automatically. Its programming tells it what to do. Robots do work that is hard or dangerous for people to do. They can do jobs even where there is no air. Robots also do things that can be too boring for people to do.

Question:

_____
_____

Answer:
_____
_____
_____
_____

2 Most robots stay in one spot and have a moving arm that lifts things or uses a tool. Robots you see every day include automatic doors, automatic car washes, and automatic teller machines. Other robots work in factories making things like computer chips and cars. Mobile robots use sensors and cameras to move around. Mobile robots have been used to map the ocean floor and the surface of Mars.

Question:

_____
_____

Answer:
_____
_____
_____
_____

3 A robot has a control center, which is a computer or part of a computer. The computer stores the robot's instructions. These instructions tell the robot how to do a job. The computer tells the robot's joints to move. Then motors cause the robot to move.

Question:

_____
_____

Answer:
_____
_____
_____
_____

Compare and Contrast

Name _____

Date _____

Choose ___ or more activities to do.
When you finish an activity, color its number.

---

1 | Contrast two book characters. Label a sheet of paper as shown. Complete each section by describing each character.

Buddy		Sheila
	gender	
	age	
	appearance	
	what he/she does	
	what he/she wants	
	character traits	

2 | As you read each chapter in a story, indicate how many important events occur. Connect the dots and compare the chapters.

More than 3 important events					●	
1 or 2 important events	●	●		●		
Nothing important happened.			●			
Chapter	1	2	3	4	5	6

3 | Think about how the characters in a particular story speak. Write a paragraph telling how your conversations compare to theirs.

Naw! We haven't seen hide nor hair of him.

4 | Read the first chapter of a story. Then answer the questions. Once you have finished the story, answer them again. Compare.

- Where does it take place?
- What are the main events?
- What is the main problem?
- What's your opinion of the character named _____?
- What's your opinion of the character named _____?

5 | Do the practice page "Dare to Compare."

6 | Read two different versions of a fairy tale. Write two paragraphs explaining how the stories compare and contrast.

POOF!

7 | Copy and complete the topic sentence. Then finish the paragraph, using at least five or more sentences.

_____ and _____ **are different in several ways.**

8 | Compare the products from two different magazine ads. List at least three ways the products are alike. Then list at least three ways they are different.

THE ZONE
Better Mileage
Better Ride!

Microride
Small Car
Big Value!

9 | Write a paragraph that compares and contrasts two different rooms in your home. Underline the similarities in blue. Underline the differences in green.

Choose & Do Language Arts Grids • ©The Mailbox® Books • TEC61227

Note to the teacher: Supply fairy tales for activity 6 and old magazines for activity 8. Program the student directions with the number of activities to be completed. Then copy the page and page 22 (back-to-back if desired) for each student.

21

Name _____ Date _____

Dare to Compare

Fill in the top blanks with the
  names of two famous people.
After reading about these people,
  complete each section.

I'm comparing

with

_____   _____.

first person   second person

	home and family	
	childhood activities	
	education	
	achievements	

When I compared them, I found they are alike in these ways:

Literature Response: Fiction

Name _____

Date _____

Choose ___ or more activities to do.
When you finish an activity, color its number.

1 List the name of each character in a story. Write three adjectives to describe each character.	**2** Choose a story with more than one setting. Label and illustrate a paper strip to show the different settings. Tape the ends together for display.	**3** Identify the genre of a specific story you've read. Write how you know. Provide text evidence with page numbers to support your thinking.

1 List the name of each character in a story. Write three adjectives to describe each character.

Robin Hood	brave resourceful rebellious
Friar Tuck	concerned helpful kind

2 Choose a story with more than one setting. Label and illustrate a paper strip to show the different settings. Tape the ends together for display.

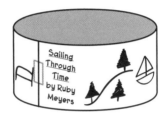

Sailing Through Time by Ruby Meyers

3 Identify the genre of a specific story you've read. Write how you know. Provide text evidence with page numbers to support your thinking.

realistic fiction   FANTASY   historical fiction

myth   mystery   folktale

This story is fantasy. I know this because...

---

4 Think about a specific story's point of view. Explain to a friend at least three ways the story would change if it was told from another character's point of view.

IF this story had been told by the **mother** instead of the **mouse**,...

5 Do the practice page "Blogging About a Book."

6 On different paper squares, write each important event in a story's plot. Add illustrations. Staple the squares sequentially to make a booklet.

---

7 Divide a sheet of paper in half. Sketch your favorite character on one side and your least favorite character on the other side. Describe the traits of each.

My Favorite Character — Samuel

My Least Favorite Character — Mr. Brown

8 Write a letter to the author of a book you enjoyed. Describe how the book made you feel. Write about the main message you got from the story.

Dear ~

9 Copy this chart and use it to rate a book. Explain each rating in complete sentences using evidence from the book.

Category	1 (low)–5 (high)	Explanation
plot		
characters		
writing style		
mood		
illustrations		

Choose & Do Language Arts Grids • ©The Mailbox® Books • TEC61227

Note to the teacher: Program student directions with the number of activities to be completed. Then copy the page and page 24 (back-to-back if desired) for each student.

23

Literature Response: Fiction

Name _____ Date _____

Blogging About a Book

Choose one important event from a story.
Write a brief blog entry about it. Ask a friend to write a response to your post.

http://www.ilovebooks.web   Search

A Highlight From _____
                              book title

illustration of the event

caption

Response to "A Highlight"

Posted by _____

Book's author:

Posted by _____

Informational Text

Read all about it!

Name _____

Date _____

Choose ____ or more activities to do.
When you finish an activity, color its number.

---

1 Scan a magazine. Write to explain each of the following:

- title and purpose
- who will want to read it
- reasons why people will want to read it
- steps to take to subscribe to it
- articles it contains

2 Copy and complete the chart below for the text you're reading.

Item	Page Number
table of contents	
glossary	
graph or chart	
map or diagram	
subheadings	
boldfaced word	
photo	

3 Choose a recipe. Write its title. Then list, in order, the verbs that describe the steps. Repeat for a second recipe.

Tamale Pie
1. preheat
2. cook
3. stir
4. drain
5. mix
6. spread
7. sprinkle
8. bake

---

4 Explain how the main idea of a news article is related to its title. Find three examples. Write each main idea with its title.

TITLE

Main Idea

5 Do the practice page "Read All About It!"

6 Write captions for ten pictures. Share the pictures and your captions with a friend. Find out if your pal would have written a similar caption.

An erupting volcano threatens a remote village.

Teens bring smiles to the faces of seniors during a sing-along.

---

7 Choose two graphs from a text. Answer these questions about each graph.

- **What is the graph's title?**
- **What information is shown on the X-axis? on the Y-axis?**
- **What are two of the main ideas of this graph?**

8 Find examples of text organized in two of the ways below. List where you found your examples.

- **events in order**
- **descriptions**
- **comparing or contrasting**
- **causes and effects**
- **problems and solutions**

9 Locate two informational books or news articles. Complete the following graphic organizer for each text.

Title or heading:

Subheading: | Subheading: | Subheading:

Main idea from first paragraph:

Main idea from last paragraph:

Choose & Do Language Arts Grids • ©The Mailbox® Books • TEC61227

Note to the teacher: Supply magazines, newspapers, cookbooks, and other informational texts. Program the student directions with the number of activities to be completed. Then copy the page and page 26 (back-to-back, if desired) for each student.

25

Informational Text

Name _____ Date _____

Read All About It!

Write about the information you read.

Informational text I read:

A Connection I Made

Features This Text Has

- [ ] heading
- [ ] subheading
- [ ] caption
- [ ] photo
- [ ] map
- [ ] graph
- [ ] diagram
- [ ] bold print
- [ ] italic print
- [ ] sidebar

Topic of This Text

Words Worth Knowing

Meaning:

Meaning:

Meaning:

Interesting Fact

Main Idea   related

Interesting Fact

Main Idea   related

What I wonder now:

Homophones

Name _____

Date _____

Dramatic Sale on Moonlight Sails

Choose ____ or more activities to do.
When you finish an activity, color its number.

1 Copy these homophone pairs. Use a dictionary to verify each word's meaning. Write each definition in your own words. **pain, pane** **vain, vane** **main, mane** **rain, reign** **plain, plane**	**2** Write a sentence that includes both words in each pair of homophones. Show that you understand each word's meaning. Circle the homophones. **be, bee** **flea, flee** **tea, tee** **meat, meet** **feat, feet**	**3** Fold a sheet of paper and then unfold it to make six sections. Illustrate and label three pairs of homophones. **pail, pale** **mail, male** **sail, sale** **tail, tale** **bail, bale**
4 Write a sentence for each homophone below, but put a blank where the homophone belongs. Ask a friend to fill in each blank. Check your pal's work. **dear, deer** **die, dye** **knight, night** **their, they're** **right, write**	**5** Do the practice page "See the Sale: Sail the Sea."  Sale! Sunset sails now half price.	**6** Match each homophone pair. Draw a picture to show what each word means. eight steel steak heel real gait break steal ate gate heal stake brake reel
7 Unscramble each homophone pair. Then write one sentence for each pair.  Pour clean, soapy water on that poor, dirty dog. rouf, rof eros, arso keap, epek kwea, kwee	**8** Write a rhyming poem using at least four of the following homophone pairs: **pair, pear** **fair, fare** **hair, hare** **stair, stare** **blew, blue** **threw, through**	**9** Write a story about a king. Use at least three of the following pairs of homophones: **thrown, throne** **groan, grown** **loan, lone** **moan, mown** **allowed, aloud** 

Choose & Do Language Arts Grids • ©The Mailbox® Books • TEC61227 • Key p. 91

Note to the teacher: Program the student directions with the number of activities to be completed. Then copy the page and page 28 (back-to-back if desired) for each student.

27

Name _____

Date _____

Homophones

See the Sale: Sail the Sea

Fill in the blank to complete each sentence.
Write the corresponding letter beside the numeral.

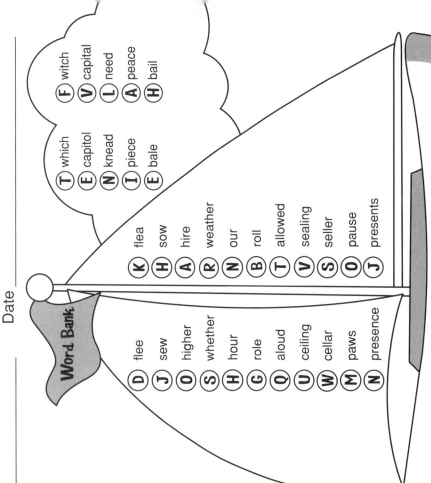

Word Bank

(T) which	(F) witch	(D) flee	(K) flea
(E) capitol	(V) capital	(J) sew	(H) sow
(N) knead	(L) need	(O) higher	(A) hire
(I) piece	(A) peace	(S) whether	(R) weather
(E) bale	(H) bail	(H) hour	(N) our
		(G) role	(B) roll
		(Q) aloud	(T) allowed
		(U) ceiling	(V) sealing
		(W) cellar	(S) seller
		(M) paws	(O) pause
		(N) presence	(J) presents

1. Your _____ is required in the principal's office.

2. Mom wants me to _____ my game for a minute.

3. _____ costume will you wear?

4. There's just an _____ left before we leave.

5. Save a _____ of cake for your sister.

6. You must _____ the dough and then let it rise.

7. I'll play the _____ of the banker.

8. I think it's easy to _____ a button on a shirt.

9. He'll paint the _____ using a roller with a long handle.

10. I don't know _____ to go or not.

11. Talking is not _____ in the library.

12. Store the potatoes in the _____ where it's cool.

13. Maybe the company will _____ Dad for the job.

14. The _____ of our state is five miles from here.

15. A _____ of hay can be very heavy.

16. Seagulls _____ when people come close.

What did the water say to the boat?
To solve the riddle, write each letter on its
matching numbered line.

It __ __ __ __ __ __ __ .
   1 2 3 4 5 6 7

__ __ __ __ __ __ __ __ __ .
8 9 10 11 12 13 14 15 16

Note to the teacher: Use with page 27.

Idioms

It's a **piece of cake!**

As **easy as pie!**

Name _____

Date _____

Choose ___ or more activities to do.
When you finish an activity, color its number.

1 Fold a paper strip into thirds. Trim the corners to create an egg shape. Unfold. Copy an idiom from below onto each egg. On the back, explain the meaning of each idiom. Don't count your chickens before they hatch. Don't put all your eggs in one basket. You're no spring chicken.	**2** Which idiom doesn't fit in this group? Write to explain what each one means and why one doesn't fit. • under the weather • run out of steam • up a creek without a paddle • bite off more than you can chew • give one's right arm	**3** Sort these idioms under the headings "happy" and "unhappy." Write sentences using two idioms from each column. • crack me up • hot under the collar • a chip on your shoulder • fit to be tied • on cloud nine • drive her up the wall • as pleased as punch • get up on the wrong side of the bed
4 Fold and unfold a sheet of paper to create four spaces. Copy each idiom below in a space. Draw a picture of the idiom's literal meaning. Then write to explain what it really means. **It's raining cats and dogs.** **You're the apple of my eye.** **I'll see that when pigs fly.** **He lost his head.**	**5** Do the practice page "Chicken Chatter." 	**6** Choose an idiom. Relate it to one of the characters or events from your current reading. Explain to a friend how the idiom fits the story. **She's mad as a hornet.** **He had an axe to grind.** **She cried wolf.** **He hit the nail on the head.** **That was the last straw.**
7 Have you experienced the things below? Copy each idiom. Then write *yes* or *no* next to it. Write a short personal story about one. **had a taste of your own medicine** **have beaten around the bush** **have been saved by the bell** **had to start from scratch**	**8** Design a card for someone you know. Use at least one idiom in the message.  I hear you've been under the weather. It was music to my ears to hear your news.	**9** Create a flip book. Copy an idiom onto each flap and illustrate its literal meaning. Under each flap, explain what the idiom really means. I was barking up the wrong tree. She's in the doghouse. His bark is worse than his bite.  looking in the wrong place

Choose & Do Language Arts Grids • ©The Mailbox® Books • TEC61227 • Key p. 91

Note to the teacher: Program the student directions with the number of activities to be completed. Then copy the page and page 30 (back-to-back if desired) for each student.

Name _____

Date _____

Idioms

Chicken Chatter

Write the letter of the definition that matches the idiom in each sentence.

I'm not sure this place is all it's cracked up to be!

1. I hear that the farmhand works for **chicken feed.**

2. No money is left over for a **nest egg.**

3. Don't **have a cow.** I'm coming!

4. She sent me on a **wild goose chase.**

5. I didn't mean to **let the cat out of the bag.**

6. **Hold your horses!** We'll get there soon enough.

7. That rooster will crow **until the cows come home** for the barn.

8. He always **makes a beeline for** the barn.

9. I would be a **fish out of water** in the city.

10. If you want to get your way, you had better **take the bull by the horns.**

11. I heard it **straight from the horse's mouth.**

12. It really **gets my goat** when people are rude.

13. Once he was caught stealing, **his goose was cooked.**

14. I'm afraid you **put the cart before the horse.**

a. annoys me

b. was in big trouble

c. a very small amount of money

d. a pointless search

e. reveal a secret

f. move in a straight line toward

g. feel uncomfortable in a strange place

h. face a challenge boldly

i. did things in the wrong order

j. money to save

k. get upset

l. from the one who knows

m. be patient

n. for a very long time

Choose & Do Language Arts Grids • ©The Mailbox® Books • TEC61227 • Key p. 91

Note to the teacher: Use with page 29.

Similes and Metaphors

Name _____

Date _____

Choose ___ or more activities to do.
When you finish an activity, color its number.

1 Use the words below to create similes that describe animals. Then create four more similes about animals. Example: My little brother is as sneaky as a snake. **sneaky spry** **SHOWY prickly** **noisy watchful**	**2** Read several poems. List the similes and metaphors you find. Illustrate your favorite. Similes Metaphors	**3** Look through advertisements for examples of metaphors and similes. List at least four. Share your list with a friend. 
4 Think of a characteristic of each fruit below. Write a simile for each fruit. Then write similes for six vegetables. **apple orange pineapple** **peach lemon watermelon** That pineapple is as sweet as my Great Aunt Sofie!	**5** Do the practice page "How About That Ride?" 	**6** As you read a story, record the similes you find on one side of your paper and the metaphors on the other. Add to the list daily. 
7 Pretend a classmate is confused about the difference between a metaphor and a simile. Explain the difference in writing, using your own words.	**8** Write a letter to your best friend to tell her about the great day you just had. Include at least three similes and three metaphors in your letter. 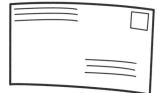	**9** Think of a specific place that fits each description below. Write a simile using each word. Then write similes for six more locations. as _____ as _____ rocky windblown sandy mountainous grassy dry as <u>swampy</u> as <u>the Everglades</u>

Choose & Do Language Arts Grids • ©The Mailbox® Books • TEC61227

Note to the teacher: Supply an assortment of poems for activity 2 and advertisements for activity 3. Program the student directions with the number of activities to be completed. Then copy the page and page 32 (back-to-back if desired) for each student.

31

Similes and Metaphors

Name _____   Date _____

How About That Ride?

Underline each simile and metaphor.
Color the ticket beside each sentence containing a metaphor yellow.

L 1. Jeremy's brain was a battlefield. Should he ride or not?

R 2. My sister, on the other hand, got a place in line as quick as a wink.

E 3. "This ride is a rocket. You'll love it!" I tried to reassure Jeremy.

X 4. As we were climbing that first hill, my sister was shaking like a leaf.

F 5. She quivered like a bowl of gelatin as she grabbed the safety bar.

C 6. I have to admit, my heart was also racing like a rabbit!

M 7. The noise was as loud as a locomotive when we went around curves.

S 8. At the highest point, my cousin, Harry, turned as white as a sheet.

W 9. Tyrell revealed that Mom cried like a baby until the very end.

D 10. She claimed the log flume was as high as Mount Everest.

A 11. Oddly, the hyena in the seat behind me couldn't stop laughing.

B 12. We shot forward like a bullet after teetering for a second at the very top.

O 13. When we finally leveled out, the noise around us was an avalanche.

V 14. All I could hear was people cackling like hens as we came to a sudden halt.

T 15. Where's a mirror? I have to see this sopping wet haystack on my head.

G 16. Look at Melissa! She's as wet as a fish.

Y 17. Hey! How did Harry manage to stay as dry as toast?

W 18. That log ride was a pleasure cruise. Let's go again!

What gets wetter and wetter the more it dries?

To solve the riddle, unscramble the letters from the yellow tickets and write the answer on the lines.

___ ___ ___ ___ ___ ___ ___ ___

Choose & Do Language Arts Grids • ©The Mailbox® Books • TEC61227 • Key p. 91

Multiple-Meaning Words/Homographs

Name _____

Date _____

Choose ___ or more activities to do.
When you finish an activity, color its number.

1 Write a paragraph using the words below. Use each word twice to show two different meanings.
 	
bat *chest*
 	
down
 	
hose **light**
	2 Write a riddle for each word below.
	
	palm trip wave
	pen ruler fly
	play land
	
	I am part of an elephant or the part of a car that holds a spare tire. *(trunk)*
		3 Write a sentence using each word below as a verb.
		
		subject
		  record
		perfect
		  contract
		convict

4 Draw sketches to show two different meanings for each word below. tire swing ball **park** roll	**5** Do the practice page "Tricksters' Prank." SOMETHING SPECIAL FOR YOU!	**6** Write a sentence using each word below as a noun. bass wave **down** ground fine bark
7 Draw four columns and write each word below in the first one. In the other columns, write different meanings for each word. hand fan tackle land ground pass <table><tr><td>hand</td><td></td><td></td><td></td></tr><tr><td>land</td><td></td><td></td><td></td></tr><tr><td>fan</td><td></td><td></td><td></td></tr></table>	**8** Use each word below in two sentences to show two different meanings. ship watch point second stuff right	**9** Write a sentence using each word below as a verb. Then write a sentence using it as a noun. **tear** **coast** **trip** **content** **wind** **produce**

Choose & Do Language Arts Grids • ©The Mailbox® Books • TEC61227 • Key p. 91

Note to the teacher: Program the student directions with the number of activities to be completed. Then copy the page and page 34 (back-to-back if desired) for each student.

Multiple-Meaning Words/Homographs

Tricksters' Prank

And sometimes they have *different* pronunciations.

Homographs are tricksters.

They are spelled the same but have *different* meanings.

Write, in order, each letter you circled.

_____

_____

What's in the lovely package?
To find out, unscramble each word onto the lines.

Circle the letter beside the meaning that matches each underlined homograph.

1. He put a glossy <u>finish</u> on the table.
   r   to bring to an end
   s   to use entirely
   t   final coat on a surface

2. When it was time to speak, he forgot his <u>lines</u>.
   f   strong slender cords
   g   to cover the inner surface
   h   words a character speaks in a play

3. She had to <u>face</u> the fact that he was gone.
   n   front part of the human head
   o   recognize and deal with
   p   the front, upper, or outer surface

4. Use a magnifying glass to see that <u>minute</u> insect.
   c   very small
   d   sixty seconds
   e   a brief note

5. Miniature golf is a <u>game</u> of precision.
   r   animals taken in hunting
   s   activity for amusement
   t   number of points necessary to win

6. He likes to <u>spring</u> out from behind doors to scare me.
   j   a source of water from the ground
   k   a tightly wound cord
   l   leap or jump suddenly

7. <u>Clear</u> away the dishes and run the dishwasher.
   o   transparent
   p   to remove things
   q   bright, cloudless

8. The new fence will <u>run</u> parallel with the road.
   h   to enter an election
   i   to take a certain direction
   j   a score made in baseball

9. He waved his baton to <u>conduct</u> the orchestra.
   e   to lead
   f   to transmit electricity
   g   a standard of behavior

10. The roof had an unusually steep <u>pitch</u>.
    k   degree of slope
    l   highness or lowness of sound
    m   sales talk

Note to the teacher: Use with page 33.

Synonyms and Antonyms

Name _____

Date _____

Choose ___ or more activities to do.
When you finish an activity, color its number.

1 Copy the pairs of words. Label each pair as synonyms or antonyms.

calm, nervous	flower, bloom
bumpy, rough	light, dark
red, scarlet	play, work
laugh, cry	speak, talk

2 Write each of the following words in the center of a flower that has five petals. On each flower, write a synonym on each petal. Use a thesaurus. Color.

good
big
small
run
say
wonder

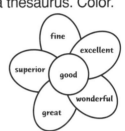

3 Write each word in the middle of an index card. Print six antonyms around the edges of the card.

joy
filthy
timid
enemy
ordinary
lazy

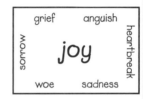

4 Copy and rewrite each sentence twice, changing the underlined word first to a synonym and then to an antonym.

I decided to wear a plain shirt.
My mom cried at the movie.
The boy's pace was slow.
You did a fine job on the test.
Can workers repair the fence?

5 Do the practice page "Gabbing About the Garden."

6 Identify which pairs of words are synonyms and which are antonyms. Write them under the correct headings.

depart	sweet	speedy
tasty	nervous	low
high	shout	sugary
quick	delicious	cowardly
brave	calm	yell
	arrive	

7 Copy each word on a card. Make an antonym card for each. Shuffle. Turn the cards facedown. Play Memory with a friend. Locate the matching cards.

interesting	arrive	yell
panic	angry	important
real	horrible	

8 Copy the paragraph. Circle at least five overused words. Edit to include synonyms that would improve the passage. Use a thesaurus.

It was a nice day for a walk. Looking at the garden, we saw pretty colors. A big cloud caused us to run for shelter. We got wet anyway.

9 Use a dictionary and a thesaurus to find synonyms and antonyms for each of these three words. Which of your lists is longest? Discuss it with a friend.

happy		huge		help	
S	A	S	A	S	A

Note to the teacher: Program the student directions with the number of activities to be completed. Then copy the page and page 36 (back-to-back if desired) for each student.

Synonyms and Antonyms

Name _____   Date _____

Gabbing About the Garden

Lightly shade a seed to show whether the words in each pair are antonyms, synonyms, or neither.

	antonyms	synonyms	neither
1. sow, harvest	G	S	H
2. sprout, germinate	T	G	P
3. moist, dry	C	E	T
4. forecast, predict	Y	A	S
5. sow, plant	F	R	N
6. fungus, fertilize	S	O	D
7. ripen, mature	C	D	W
8. harvest, gather	Q	E	Z
9. shovel, hoe	M	W	V
10. cultivate, plow	E	N	O
11. shallow, deep	H	V	U
12. transplant, move	I	H	G
13. dig, weeds	L	C	S
14. site, location	A	O	M
15. foliage, vegetation	U	S	R
16. trim, prune	B	E	C

What kind of socks does a gardener wear?
To answer the riddle, write each shaded letter in the synonym column in order on the lines.

___ ___ ___ ___ ___ ___ ___ ___ ___ ___

Prefixes and Suffixes

Name _____

Date _____

Choose ____ or more activities to do.
When you finish an activity, color its number.

---

1 List four words for each of the prefixes below. Use a dictionary.

pre- before	re- again	mis- bad, badly	un- not

2 Copy each sentence. Circle and define the prefix in the underlined word. Write a sentence using a different word that contains the same prefix.

I work for an <u>international</u> company.
Relax and don't <u>overdo</u> it.
That singer is <u>extraordinary</u>!
Your room is <u>disorganized</u>.

3 The prefixes below relate to quantities or numbers. Use a dictionary to help you list five words for each of these prefixes.

uni- one	bi- two
tri- three	quad- four

---

4 List "before" words that use the prefixes *pre-* and *fore-*. Then list "after" words that use *post-* and *after-*. Are there related words?

pre- or fore-
before

post- or after-
after

5 Do the practice page "Take It for a Spin."

6 Putting a -*y* suffix on a word creates an **adjective**. Adding an -*ly* suffix creates an **adverb**. List eight words using each suffix.

That is a squeaky door.
Squeaky is an **adjective** modifying *door*.

She eagerly ate the pie.
Eagerly is an **adverb** telling how she ate.

---

7 The suffixes -*er* and -*or* indicate "someone who." Use a dictionary to correctly spell the term for a person who does each task below.

direct	borrow	narrate
govern	survey	examine
counsel	report	illustrate
believe	invent	visit

8 Change each word so that it has a -*tion* suffix. What part of speech is each word?

elect	subtract	attract
collect	instruct	destruct
protect	connect	predict

9 Select and list five prefixes and five suffixes from this page. Write a story that includes the listed affixes. Circle them. Illustrate your story.

Choose & Do Language Arts Grids • ©The Mailbox® Books • TEC61227 • Key p. 92

Note to the teacher: Program the student directions with the number of activities to be completed. Then copy the page and page 38 (back-to-back if desired) for each student.

37

Name _____

Date _____

Prefixes and Suffixes

Take It for a Spin

Read the words below, looking for prefixes and suffixes. Write each word on a wheel or in the middle section to indicate the word's affixes.

Words With Suffixes

Words With Prefixes and Suffixes

Words With Prefixes

Word Bank

semiconductor	postseason	homeless	poetic	cohabit
transcribe	teacher	violinist	autograph	insensitive
kingdom	decoder	capability	reactor	equidistant
		assistance	undeniably	
		discontentment	hemisphere	
			periscope	

Choose & Do Language Arts Grids • ©The Mailbox® Books • TEC61227 • Key p. 92

Note to the teacher: Use with page 37.

Greek Word Parts

Name _____

Date _____

Choose ___ or more activities to do.
When you finish an activity, color its number.

1 Choose one of the Greek word parts. Find and list at least three words made using each part. Use the words to make a word search on graph paper. **mono** **tri** **tetra** **penta**	**2** Choose one of the Greek word parts. Find and list at least four words made with that part. Use the words for one word part to make a word art picture like the one shown. **biblio** **geo** **therm** hydrant, hydrate, hydroelectric, hydr (water), hydroplane	**3** Find two words that have Greek word parts. Make a word map for each word. Word: Antarctica / Greek word part and meaning: Part of speech: / Definition: Sentence:
4 On graph paper, make a crossword puzzle featuring words made from one of the Greek word parts below. Give your puzzle to a friend to solve. *graph* = record *photo* = light *scope* = instrument for viewing *therm* = heat	**5** Do the practice page "Getting to the Root" on page 40.	**6** Cut colored paper to make a pennant. Write one of the Greek word parts and its meaning. Fill the pennant with words that include the featured part. **bio** (life): biochemical biodegradable biopsy biography biology biohazard biotic biographer biometrics biofeedback bioengineering
7 Read the sample riddle. Then create similar riddles for *exoskeleton, hydroelectric,* and *autograph*. Post the riddles where others can read them. I contain a Greek word part that means *measure*. I also contain a Greek word part that means *heat*. What am I? **Answer**: thermometer	**8** For each word, fold a sheet of paper in half and cut two slits as shown. Write the meaning of each word part beneath the corresponding flap. **geometric microscopic** **biodegradable** *prefix* root suffix	**9** Draw a spiderweb. Write one of the Greek word parts in the center with its meaning. Add a related word to each section of the web. *astro* = star *micro* = little *aero* = air *amphi* = both *photo* (light)

Choose & Do Language Arts Grids • ©The Mailbox® Books • TEC61227

Note to the teacher: Provide graph paper for activities 1 and 4. Program the student directions with the number of activities to be completed. Then copy the page and page 40 (back-to-back if desired) for each student.

39

Greek Word Parts

Name _____ Date _____

Getting to the Root

Unscramble the words.
Hint: The beginning letter of each word is in bold.
Then list each word in the correct section.

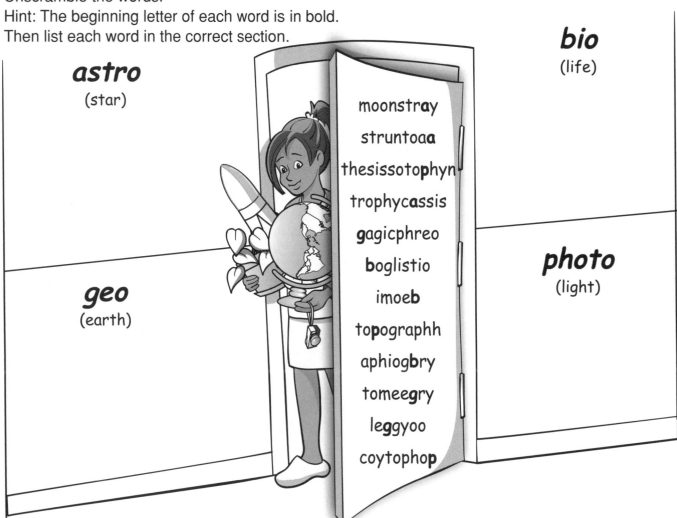

astro
(star)

bio
(life)

geo
(earth)

photo
(light)

moonstr**a**y
struntoa**a**
thesissoto**ph**yn
trophyc**a**ssis
gagicphreo
boglistio
imoe**b**
to**p**ographh
aphiog**b**ry
tomeegry
le**g**gyoo
coytopho**p**

Use three of the unscrambled words in sentences.

1. _____
   _____

2. _____
   _____

3. _____
   _____

Latin Word Parts

Name _____

Date _____

Choose ___ or more activities to do.
When you finish an activity, color its number.

---

1 Choose one of the Latin word parts. Locate at least eight words that use that word part. Use the words to make a word search on graph paper.

uni = one
bi = two
tri = three
quadri = four

2 Choose one of the Latin word parts. Locate at least eight words made with that word part. Use the words for one word part to make a word art picture like the one shown.

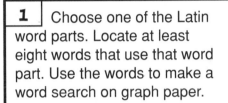

aud = hear
ped = foot
port = carry
scrib, script = write
spect = see

3 Find two words that have Latin word parts. Make a word map for each word.

Word: scribble	Latin word part and meaning:
Part of speech:	Definition:
Sentence:	

4 On graph paper, make a crossword puzzle featuring words made from one of these Latin word parts. Give your puzzle to a friend to solve.

aqua = water
sub = under
stell = star
tact = touch

5 Do the practice page "A Revealing Pattern."

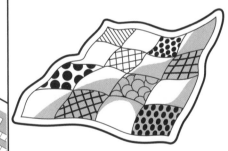

6 Cut colored paper to make a banner. Write a Latin word part and its meaning. Fill the banner with words that include the featured part.

terra
(earth)
• territory • terrestrial
• terrain • terrarium
• terrier

7 Read the sample riddle. Create similar riddles for *transport*, *manuscript*, and *television*. Post the riddles where others can read them.

I contain a Latin word part that means *to write*.
I also contain the word *crib*.
What am I?

Answer: scribble

8 For each word, fold a sheet of paper in half and cut two slits as shown. Write the meaning of each part beneath the corresponding flap.

prescription   incredible
distraction

| prefix | root | suffix |

9 Draw a spiderweb. Write one of the Latin word parts in the center with its meaning. Add a related word to each section of the web.

scrib, script = write
port = carry
spect = see

port
(to carry)

Note to the teacher: Provide graph paper for activities 1 and 4. Program the student directions with the number of activities to be completed. Then copy the page and page 42 (back-to-back if desired) for each student.

Latin Word Parts

Name _____   Date _____

A Revealing Pattern

Let me in**spect** that for you.

Choose a word part from the lower right box.
Write the part in the upper left square and its meaning in the center square.
Then fill each triangle with a word containing that word part.
Complete the remaining squares and lightly color the design.

spect

see

Latin word part selected:

The most interesting thing I notice about these words is:

The meaning of this Latin word part is:

_____
is a word I didn't know.

It means _____
_____
_____ .

Latin Word Parts

aud = hear
port = carry
meter = measure
spect = see
struct = build
scrip, scrib = write

Choose & Do Language Arts Grids • ©The Mailbox® Books • TEC61227

42   **Note to the teacher:** Use with page 41. Display several of these squares together for a quilt-like word wall.

Analogies

Choose ___ or more activities to do.
When you finish an activity, color its number.

1 Copy the analogies. Fill in the missing words from the choices below. Then write two analogies of your own.

Small is to *tiny* as *huge* is to _____.
Near is to *close* as *far* is to _____.
Tasty is to *delicious* as *hungry* is to _____.
Nervous is to *tense* as *calm* is to _____.

peaceful   giant   starving   distant

2 Fold paper to divide it into fourths and then unfold it. Copy each analogy into one section. Complete the analogy with a word below and illustrate it.

slim : fat :: thin : _____
dark : light :: night : _____
smooth : rough :: straight : _____
hot : cold :: melt : _____

freeze   curved   day   wide

3 Copy each analogy and then complete it. Write to explain the relationship in each analogy. Use the clues below.

Kittens are to cats as puppies are to _____.
Bees are to honey as cows are to _____.
Notes are to music as letters are to _____.

Clues | part to whole
young to adult
product produced by

4 Copy each analogy and then complete it. Write to explain the relationships in each analogy.

seconds : minutes :: minutes : _____

days : weeks :: months : _____

October : fall :: January : _____

Flag Day : June :: Mother's Day :: _____

5 Do the practice page "Totally in Tune."

6 Copy and correct these analogies so they make sense. Tell what was wrong and how you fixed it.

Dog is to *bark* as *cat* is to *soft*.
Inches are to *feet* as *cents* are to *miles*.
Sweet is to *sour* as *soft* is to *gentle*.

7 Copy each analogy and then complete it. Write to explain the relationships in each analogy.

candle : lantern :: lightbulb : _____

ink : pen :: paint : _____

burner : oven :: faucet : _____

8 Write five incomplete analogies using one of the relationships below. Make an answer key. Ask a friend to fill in the blanks. Discuss the answers.
- **synonyms**
- **antonyms**
- **part to whole**

finger : hand :: toe : _____

9 Copy each analogy and then complete it. Write to explain the relationships in each analogy.

Angry is to *yell* as *happy* is to _____.
Ice skater is to *rink* as *runner* is to _____.
Pear is to *fruit* as *celery* is to _____.
Gasoline is to *car* as *electricity* is to _____.

Note to the teacher: Program the student directions with the number of activities to be completed. Then copy the page and page 44 (back-to-back if desired) for each student.

43

Analogies

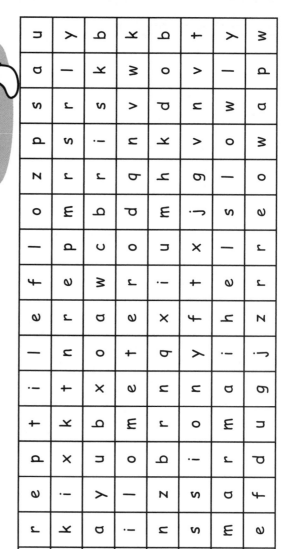

Totally in Tune

Use a word from the word bank to complete each analogy.
Circle your answers in the puzzle. Not all words will be used.

1. hammer : builder :: pencil : _____

2. feet : mile :: meters : _____

3. cow : milk :: chicken : _____

4. poodle : dog :: flamingo : _____

5. squirrel : mammal :: snake : _____

6. wolf : howl :: bird : _____

7. second : minute :: minute : _____

8. laces : shoe :: zipper : _____

9. trumpet : brass :: drums : _____

10. moist : damp :: chilly : _____

11. brave : cowardly :: swiftly : _____

12. knob : door :: faucet : _____

j	i	s	f	q	a	c	r	e	p	t	i	l	e	f	l	o	z	p	s	a	u
a	h	c	j	c	g	e	k	i	x	k	t	n	r	e	p	m	r	s	r	l	y
c	r	h	o	u	r	w	a	y	u	b	x	o	a	w	c	b	r	i	s	k	b
k	g	i	e	e	k	p	k	i	l	o	m	e	t	e	r	o	d	q	d	w	k
e	t	r	o	h	d	l	n	z	b	r	n	q	e	r	o	d	q	h	d	o	b
t	u	p	e	r	c	u	s	s	i	o	n	y	f	x	j	g	l	j	v	v	t
v	s	g	t	a	j	y	m	a	r	i	h	e	s	l	h	i	n	w	l	y	y
u	r	x	g	u	z	j	e	f	d	u	g	j	z	r	r	e	o	w	a	p	w

WORD BANK	
sink	brisk
percussion	chirp
handsome	bird
kilometer	slowly
jacket	phone
hour	reptile
egg	writer

Choose & Do Language Arts Grids • ©The Mailbox® Books • TEC61227 • Key p. 93

Note to the teacher: Use with page 43.

Capitalization

Name _____

Date _____

Choose ___ or more activities to do.
When you finish an activity, color its number.

1 Copy the sentences. Add capitals where needed. • jessica dickensen left for walt disney world last tuesday, march 17. • my grandmother taught me to play cribbage on the plane ride to florida. • i loved visiting universal studios but had the most fun swimming at daytona beach.	**2** Unscramble the words. Add capitals where needed. idfyar shtnowigan yarnauj vennpailsany neevau trovengemn dreemof fojernefs rolamime etinud sattes	**3** Read the list of book titles. Rewrite them with the appropriate words capitalized. Fables and what they mean the mystery of timber ridge a guide to making quilts the art of making tackles
4 Write a proper noun for each of the common nouns listed. Use capitals where needed. **teacher doctor** **building company** **team movie** **street magazine**	**5** Do the practice page "Touring the National Mall." 	**6** Write a paragraph without any capitalization. Trade your paragraph with a friend who's also doing this activity. Correct your pal's work. 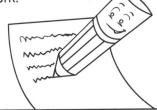
7 Create a poster that explains when to capitalize letters in words. 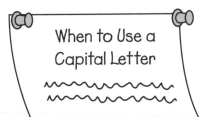 When to Use a Capital Letter	**8** Copy the address and insert capitals where they belong. Then write your own address with appropriate capitals. tessier and sons, inc. 42 pine crest lane gingerville, ma 40511	**9** Label a page as shown. Copy each word below into the correct column. Add capital letters where needed. Then add five more words in each column. motorcycle honda jacob america spanish cell phone kansas amazon brazil monument harriet arbor day | Common Nouns	Proper Nouns	 |---|---| |		

Note to the teacher: Program the student directions with the number of activities to be completed. Then copy the page and page 46 (back-to-back if desired) for each student.

Name _____ Date _____

Touring the National Mall

Draw a box around each word below that needs a capital letter.
Then color the boxes by the code.

start your tour at the lincoln memorial. inside you'll find a huge statue of abraham lincoln. our sixteenth president, author of the gettysburg address, seems to be looking past the washington monument to the capitol building. as you walk, you will go down the steps from which dr. martin luther king jr. made his most famous speech in 1963. beyond the lincoln memorial, you will find the vietnam veterans memorial. you will also see the korean war veterans memorial. stop next at the national world war ii memorial near the washington monument.

next you will approach the monument that honors our first president, george washington. there you'll see the flags that fly around its base. ride an elevator to the observation area. at the top, you will have a great view of the capitol building and the white house. to the south, you can see many cherry trees. nearby, the jefferson memorial honors the third president of the united states, thomas jefferson. he was also the author of the declaration of independence.

Free DC Walking Tours

Color Code

orange
names of people

green
first words in sentences

blue
historic events, documents, speeches

yellow
places (countries, bodies of water, buildings, monuments)

Sentence Basics

declarative

interrogative

exclamatory

imperative

Name _____

Date _____

Choose ___ or more activities to do.
When you finish an activity, color its number.

1 Copy each sentence and punctuate it. Then rewrite each declarative sentence as a question and each question as a declarative sentence.

- Gymnastics is a popular sport
- Men compete in six events
- Women compete in four events
- Which gymnastic event is your favorite

2 Copy and punctuate each sentence. Then write what type of sentence it is.

- Makayla leaps, turns, and flips on the balance beam
- Will you compete in the floor exercises
- What is her best event so far
- Wow, his performance on the rings was perfect

3 Turn these fragments into complete sentences. Add punctuation.

- the gymnastics team
- reached up for the bar
- if his hands began to slip
- leaps onto the beam

4 Unscramble each sentence and write it with correct punctuation.

- to perform their the music gymnasts of choice
- only country it gymnasts qualify why is that two from each may
- longer than are you 90 sure the routine seconds can't be
- the horse with he pommel touch knows hands he must only his

5 Do the practice page "Top-Notch Competitor."

GOLD

6 Tell whether each sentence is a fragment or a run-on. Rewrite to improve each one.

- He held the pose four seconds but then he flipped and raised his hands and he smiled.
- She kept tumbling and leaping she danced with a smile down to the last second.
- When we went home.
- Because uneven bars are her best event.

7 Find the fragments below. Use each one to write a complete sentence.

- Why are the other teams?
- Your body must be flexible to do this flip.
- Because she performs it better than the others.
- Courage to attempt difficult moves like flips.

8 Write a complete sentence for each of the four sentence types. Use the words below.

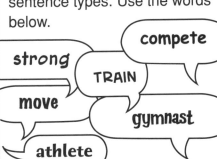

compete

strong

TRAIN

move

gymnast

athlete

9 Rewrite the run-on sentence to improve it.

When Mary Lou Retton took home the gold medal from the 1984 Olympics, Americans began to be more interested in gymnastics and boys and girls in the United States started trying it for themselves.

Choose & Do Language Arts Grids • ©The Mailbox® Books • TEC61227 • Key p. 93

Note to the teacher: Program the student directions with the number of activities to be completed. Then copy the page and page 48 (back-to-back if desired) for each student.

47

Name _____

Date _____

Sentence Basics

Top-Notch Competitor

Read each sentence.
Fill in each blank using the key.

KEY
complete sentence = C
fragment = F
run-on = R

Use each fragment on the left to write a complete sentence.

_____

_____

_____

_____

_____

_____

Edit the run-on sentences on the left by adding punctuation and capital letters.

1. ____ When she started taking classes at seven years old.

2. ____ Jenn has been taking gymnastics for three years.

3. ____ Before Jenn took lessons, she couldn't even do a somersault soon she was rolling and flipping all over the gym.

4. ____ At her first competition.

5. ____ She didn't win a medal Jenn didn't do very well at all.

6. ____ But she didn't give up Jenn worked harder instead.

7. ____ She practiced every day.

8. ____ Watched other gymnasts.

9. ____ Today she has 37 medals for her gymnastic skills.

10. ____ Jenn says gymnastics helped her see the benefit of hard work.

Note to the teacher: Use with page 47.

Subjects and Predicates

Name _____

Date _____

Choose ___ or more activities to do.
When you finish an activity, color its number.

---

1 Copy the sentences below. Circle the **simple subject** and underline the **complete subject**.

- Strawberry farms are located across the state.
- Local farmers supply grocery stores and restaurants.
- A fresh cup of berries has only 60 calories.
- Strawberries are high in Vitamin C.

2 Use the text below to combine a **subject** and a **predicate**. Write each complete sentence you make.

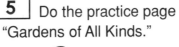

Dairy farmers	can get food and water all day
Most dairy cows	gets cleaned often
Milking equipment	make sure their cows are healthy

3 Copy the sentences below. Circle the **simple predicate (verb)** and underline the **complete predicate** in each sentence.

- Some tractors harvest corn from the field.
- A baler compresses hay into bales.
- Farmers use tractors that plant seeds.

---

4 Add a **predicate** to each **subject** below. Write the sentences.

Tomato plants
Dried cornstalks
Long, tangled pumpkin vines
Plump, juicy tomatoes

5 Do the practice page "Gardens of All Kinds."

6 Add a **subject** to each **predicate** below. Write the sentences.

- ripened quicker than I predicted
- filled the farmers' market crates
- tasted especially good this year
- were delivered to the market just in time

---

7 Rewrite the following sentences to have **compound subjects**.

The bean plants need water.
The squash is ready for harvesting.
Dean will bale the hay.

> Corn is grown around here.
> Corn and wheat are grown around here.

8 Rewrite the following sentences to have **compound predicates**.

- He plows the field.
- The tractor sputters down the row.
- Field hands pick the beans.

> Jacob plants corn.
> Jacob plants and irrigates corn.

9 Develop the simple subjects and simple predicates into **complete subjects and predicates**. Use them in five sentences.

Simple Subjects	Simple Predicates
farmer	harvests
tractor	plows
farm	sows
farm hand	transports
gardener	produces

Note to the teacher: Program the student directions with the number of activities to be completed. Then copy the page and page 50 (back-to-back if desired) for each student.

Subjects and Predicates

Name _____   Date _____

Gardens of All Kinds

Underline the complete subject and double underline the complete predicate.
Circle the simple subject and simple predicate.

1. (Mr. Jessup) my neighbor, (planted) a crop of corn in his backyard.

2. My mother buys ears of corn by the dozen.

3. The yellow corn is delicious.

4. Dad eats corn on the cob with lots of butter on it.

5. Missy, my classmate, planted flower bulbs in her yard last fall.

6. You can find flower bulbs at garden centers in the late summer.

7. She showed us the most beautiful gladiolas from her garden.

8. Missy's fourth-grade teacher was delighted with the flowers Missy gave her.

9. All plants require sunlight, water, air, and nutrients from the soil.

10. Seed packet labels tell how old the seeds are.

11. Some gardeners transplant seedlings into their gardens.

12. Gardening takes time and patience.

Write a sentence about a gardener you know. Circle the simple subject and simple predicate.

_____

_____

Subject-Verb Agreement

Name _____

Date _____

Choose ____ or more activities to do.
When you finish an activity, color its number.

---

1 Choose a singular subject to go with each singular verb below. Use the pair to write a sentence.

lion tigers monkey chimpanzees boas python sharks trout	**Singular Verbs** climbs swims prowls slithers

2 Choose a plural verb to go with each plural noun. Use the word pair to write a sentence.

saxophone harps drums trumpets flute xylophones clarinet	**Plural Verbs** beat blare lull ring

3 Choose two subjects to make a compound subject. Match them with a predicate. Write a sentence.

Subjects		
backhoes	cars	trains
tractor trailers	trucks	bulldozers

Predicates
clog the highway
carry cargo   move dirt

---

4 Find the incorrect sentences below. Rewrite them with plural verbs.

- Squirrels and birds lives in the oak.
- Bats and moths is nocturnal.
- The chipmunk and squirrel store food.
- The willow and the maple drops their leaves.
- The goat and sheep grazes on the hill.

5 Do the practice page "'Purr-fectly' Agreeable."

6 Copy each sentence. Underline the simple subject once. Underline the verb twice. Explain why the verb varies.

A cat licks its fur.
Ferrets lick their fur.
Kittens and cats lick their fur.

A dogwood sways in the wind.
Pines sway in the wind.
Maples and birches sway in the wind.

---

7 Underline the subjects and verbs. Rewrite the sentences with different verbs to correct them.

One of those trees are dead.
The dog with fleas are gone.
Our ride to the mountains were restful.
Songs like that one is upbeat.

8 Add a verb or verb phrase to each collective subject to create a sentence. Underline the verb used.

team
class
family
staff

9 Choose a verb that agrees with each compound subject. Write the corrected sentence.

A crayon or pen (work, works) for this project.
Her notebook or workbook (is, are) in the drawer.
A banana or pear (make, makes) a good snack.
His backpack or bookbag (is, are) in the locker.

Choose & Do Language Arts Grids • ©The Mailbox® Books • TEC61227 • Key p. 94

Note to the teacher: Program the student directions with the number of activities to be completed. Then copy the page and page 52 (back-to-back if desired) for each student.

51

Subject-Verb Agreement

"Purr-fectly" Agreeable

Underline the simple subject in each sentence.
Circle *S* if it is singular and *P* if it is plural.
Write a verb from the word bank to match the subject.

Meerkats	rock!		
plural subject	plural verb		

S P **1.** Scent, sound, and body language
_____ ways meerkats communicate.

S P **2.** Sand and a tumbleweed _____ all it
can see.

S P **3.** Curved front claws _____ dirt in
search of food.

S P **4.** A flock of birds _____ as it passes
overhead.

S P **5.** Guards _____ to warn others.

S P **6.** An army of ants _____ across the log.

S P **7.** The weary guard _____ for help.

S P **8.** An older adult _____ the little ones.

S P **9.** Grooming and wrestling _____
favorite pastimes.

S P **10.** The rain _____ on the parched sand.

S P **11.** A snake _____ silently past the cactus.

S P **12.** An eagle and a jackal _____ animals
to avoid.

S P **13.** A scorpion and a cricket _____ a
tasty meal.

S P **14.** A mob of meerkats _____ below for
the danger to pass.

S P **15.** Ground squirrels and mongooses
_____ their den.

S P **16.** A meerkat _____ into its den.

Word Bank

slithers	slither
beeps	beep
is	are
babysits	babysit
shares	share
is	are
signals	signal
is	are
glides	glide
shovels	shovel
splashes	splash
dives	dive
waits	wait
becomes	become
is	are
marches	march

Den, Sweet Den

Did you find an equal number of singular and plural subjects?

Choose & Do Language Arts Grids • ©The Mailbox® Books • TEC61227 • Key p. 94

Simple and Compound Sentences

Name _____

Date _____

Choose ___ or more activities to do.
When you finish an activity, color its number.

1 Unscramble each simple sentence and write it correctly. Underline the complete subject once and the complete predicate twice. • predicate and a sentence a a subject has simple • sentences two at sentence a compound contains least simple	**2** Read one or more sports articles. Copy three simple and three compound sentences. Underline the complete subjects once and the complete predicates twice. 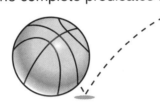	**3** Change each compound sentence into two simple sentences. Underline the complete subjects once and the complete predicates twice. • The Statue of Liberty holds a torch in her right hand, and she grasps a tablet in her left hand. • The Liberty Bell was rung at the first public reading of the Declaration of Independence, but it cracked badly on Washington's Birthday in 1846.
4 Change each simple sentence into a compound sentence. • A hurricane is forecasted. • An unusually late frost damaged crops. • The area had experienced drought.	**5** Do the practice page "Storm Watch." 	**6** Label cards with the words below. Shuffle the cards and stack them facedown. Draw a card. Use the word to make a simple sentence and then a compound one. Repeat three more times. precipitation · fog · cloud · frost · showers · rain · wind · temperature · morning
7 Write three simple and three compound sentences about your favorite school subject. Simple Sentence <u>Our music teacher</u> <u>shows us how to play rhythms.</u> Compound Sentence <u>We</u> <u>make the beat with our bodies</u>, and <u>we</u> <u>take turns playing the drums.</u>	**8** Write four compound sentences about the selections you would order at your favorite restaurant. I want to order a milk shake, but I can't drink it all. I'll have a foot-long hot dog, and fries sound good too.	**9** Write four compound sentences about dogs on paper strips, leaving spaces for conjunctions. Attach conjunctions written on bone cutouts. Labs are popular pets, {but} they can be terrible chewers. Collies are herding dogs, {and} they tend to bark a lot.

Choose & Do Language Arts Grids • ©The Mailbox® Books • TEC61227 • Key p. 94

Note to the teacher: Provide sports articles for activity 2. Program the student directions with the number of activities to be completed. Then copy the page and page 54 (back-to-back if desired) for each student.

Simple and Compound Sentences

Name _____ Date _____

Storm Watch

Use the key to label each sentence.

Key
S = simple sentence
C = compound sentence

_____ 1. Air is blowing, sinking, and rising all the time.

_____ 2. Hurricanes form over the ocean.

_____ 3. Meteorologists track storms, and they use computers to track the paths storms take.

_____ 4. Special planes are flown into storms to get information.

_____ 5. The National Weather Service tells us what to expect.

_____ 6. Broadcasts inform us of the forecast, but it's up to us to take precautions.

_____ 7. A warning means a hurricane is likely to reach land, and your next step should be to get to a safe place.

_____ 8. Bring in things like toys, flowerpots, and folding chairs.

_____ 9. Wind could pick up objects in your yard, and it could toss them toward your windows.

_____ 10. During a storm, stay inside where it is safe.

_____ 11. Storms can produce hail, and large hail can do a lot of damage.

_____ 12. Thunderstorms can happen in winter, but they are more common in warm weather.

_____ 13. Storms sometimes bring heavy rains, and the rains can cause dangerous floods.

_____ 14. Lightning strikes the tallest objects, so get down low if you're outside.

_____ 15. People are sometimes struck by lightning, but most of them survive it.

Change two of the simple sentences above into compound sentences.

• _____

_____

• _____

_____

Nouns

Name _____

Date _____

Choose ___ or more activities to do.
When you finish an activity, color its number.

1 Fold paper to create three columns. Label them as shown. Read a chapter or section from a book. Add nouns to your grid as you find them. 	**2** Sort these nouns to show whether they are common or proper. Capitalize the proper nouns.	**3** Read a news article. Underline at least 15 nouns using the key below to identify the type.

For activity 1 grid: person | place | thing

For activity 2:
NEW YORK CITY   SCHOOL
COUNTRY   MUSEUM
STATUE OF LIBERTY LIBERTY BELL
SACAGAWEA   CHOCOLATE
AQUARIUM   MARS
HOLIDAY   UNITED STATES

For activity 3:
Key
green = common
red = proper

4 Make these nouns plural. Check your spelling with a dictionary.	**5** Do the practice page "Bright Ideas."	**6** Write the irregular plural nouns for these words.

Activity 4 words:
beach   dish   catch
loaf   mix   fox
dress   wolf   echo
brush   buzz   hero

Activity 6 words:
sheep   child   ox
person   tooth   foot
woman   deer   goose
mouse   moose

7 Write a singular possessive noun to reword each of the following phrases.	**8** Write a plural possessive noun to reword each of the following phrases.	**9** Locate 12 possessive nouns in a text of your choice. List them. Label each one as plural or singular.

Activity 7 phrases:
drawing of Michael
glow of the moon
color of the grass
work of Lisa
eye of the hurricane
rim of the glass

snowboard of Zaden = Zaden's snowboard

Activity 8 phrases:
jobs of parents
homes of people
eyes of the children
labels of boxes
keys of pianos
recipes of chefs

sounds of the bugles = bugles' sounds

Choose & Do Language Arts Grids • ©The Mailbox® Books • TEC61227 • Key p. 94

Note to the teacher: Program the student directions with the number of activities to be completed. Then copy the page and page 56 (back-to-back if desired) for each student.

Name _____

Date _____

Nouns

Bright Ideas

Write the words from the bulb in the correct spaces in the chart.

Bulb words: store, Thomas Edison, General Electric, Macy's, Franklin Roosevelt, company, city, inventor, The World Dictionary of Science, president, state, New Jersey, book, Menlo Park

These nouns relate to the story of the electric lightbulb.

Common Nouns		Proper Nouns
people		
places		
things		

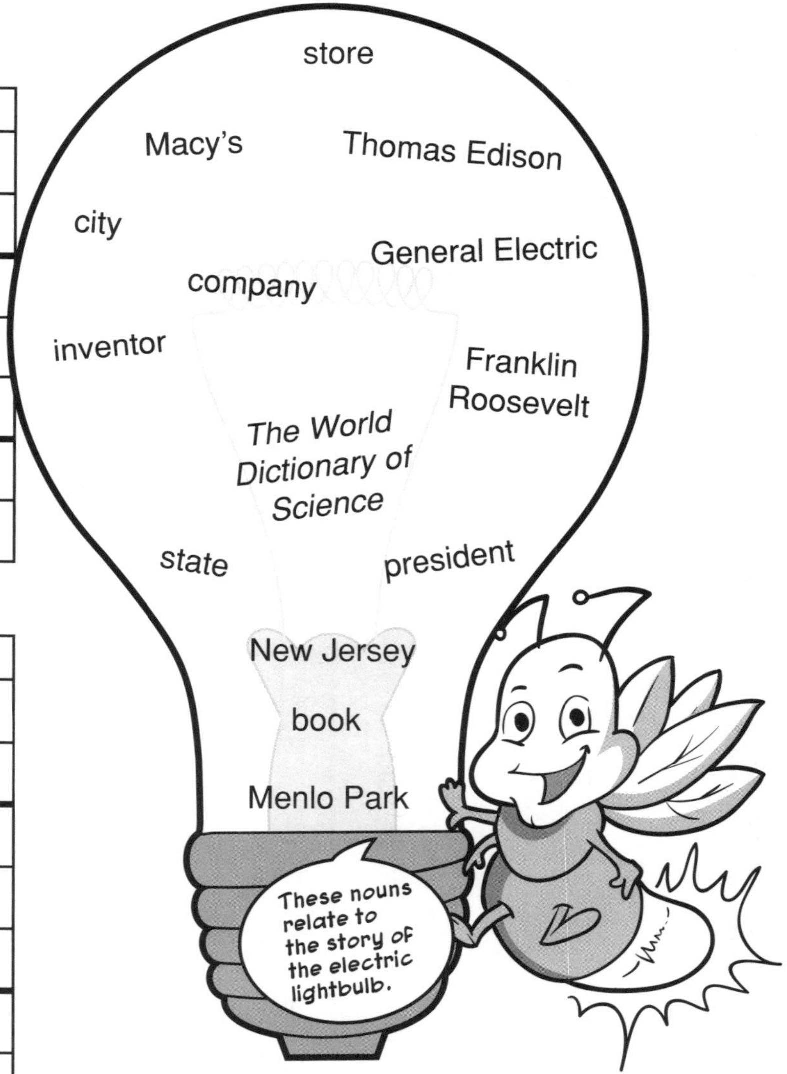

Read about a topic of your choice.
Complete the chart below with nouns related to that topic.

Common Nouns		Proper Nouns
people		
places		
things		

Choose & Do Language Arts Grids • ©The Mailbox® Books • TEC61227 • Key p. 94

Note to the teacher: Use with page 55.

Types of Verbs

Name _____

Date _____

Choose ____ or more activities to do.
When you finish an activity, color its number.

1 Read a news article. Use the key below to mark the verbs in the article. **Key** action verbs = underline once helping verbs = underline twice linking verbs = circle	**2** Cut action verbs from newspapers and magazines. Use them to create a mini collage. WRAP	**3** Create six sentences using these linking verbs. Then write each sentence on a paper strip. Glue the strips to create a chain. **is were was are** 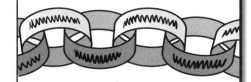
4 Use six of these verbs as linking verbs to write sentences about fast food menu items. appear feel look seem smell sound taste Those fries look greasy.	**5** Do the practice page "Cracking the Case." 	**6** Write six sentences using each of these helping verbs before main verbs. have will must can did should
7 Write a paragraph explaining the rules of your favorite game. Use each of these helping verbs. Underline the main verb you use with each of them. must can would should may will 	**8** Rewrite each sentence twice. Each time, change each verb to a more vivid or specific one. Use a thesaurus. The chipmunk ran past the door. Eagles flew overhead. She said something to him. He ate the burger.	**9** Fold a sheet of paper into three sections. Unfold it. Label each section with a heading below. Then read a story or chapter. Copy four sentences into the corresponding sections. action verbs helping verbs + main verbs linking verbs

Note to the teacher: Program the student directions with the number of activities to be completed. Then copy the page and page 58 (back-to-back if desired) for each student.

Types of Verbs

Cracking the Case

Read each sentence and underline the verb. Write the sentence number and verb on the matching file.

1. Smugly is the best in the business.

2. He is a master of disguises.

3. He will crack a case overnight.

4. The culprit ducked out of sight.

5. The crook was a slippery snake.

6. The case was solved by Smugly.

7. The butler seemed innocent.

8. Smugly began unraveling the clues.

9. The cookie snatchers were hard to nab.

10. The agents lost sight of the getaway vehicle.

11. His car sputtered to a stop.

12. The crooks were dodging Smugly.

13. Footprints led away from the crime scene.

14. Detectives can wear different disguises.

15. Smugly used a decoder ring.

Linking Verbs

Sentence ☐ _____
Sentence ☐ _____
Sentence ☐ _____
Sentence ☐ _____
Sentence ☐ _____

Helping Verbs

Sentence ☐ _____ + _____
Sentence ☐ _____ + _____
Sentence ☐ _____ + _____
Sentence ☐ _____ + _____
Sentence ☐ _____ + _____

Action Verbs

Sentence ☐ _____
Sentence ☐ _____
Sentence ☐ _____
Sentence ☐ _____
Sentence ☐ _____

Verb Tenses

Name _____

Date _____

Choose ___ or more activities to do.
When you finish an activity, color its number.

---

1 Copy the chart. Complete it by writing the past, present, and future tenses of each verb.

	Past	Present	Future
vote			
discover			
proclaim			
encourage			

2 Cut paper to make a large ribbon shape. Using regular verbs, write an alphabetical list of past and present tense verb pairs. (Skip *X*.)

The ABCs of Verb Tenses

Past Tense	Present Tense
acted	act
bumped	bump
carried	carry

U
V
W
Y
Z

3 Copy the chart. Complete it by writing the past, present, and future tenses of each of the irregular verbs.

	Past	Present	Future
steal			
take			
shrink			
fly			

---

4 Rewrite each sentence twice. Write it once in past tense and once in future tense.

Crystal jumps over the hurdle.

Derrick searches for the keys.

Sarah listens to the story.

5 Do the practice page "Our Past in the Present."

Hear ye!
Hear ye!

6 Write the irregular past tense of each verb. Use each past tense verb in a sentence.

BRING   TEACH

CATCH   KNOW

THROW   DRAW

---

7 Unscramble these irregular verbs. Then write them in the past tense.

knidr   okwn

meoc   hekas

ewar

8 Unscramble these regular verbs. Then write them in the future tense.

soatb   retinputr

mipter   leakprs

shewtli

9 Write a paragraph that tells the main things you did yesterday. Underline all the verbs. Rewrite the paragraph as though you will be doing these things in the future.

A Day in My Life

What I Did	What I Will Do

Choose & Do Language Arts Grids • ©The Mailbox® Books • TEC61227 • Key p. 95

Note to the teacher: Program the student directions with the number of activities to be completed. Then copy the page and page 60 (back-to-back if desired) for each student.

Name _____ Date _____

Our Past in the Present

Check to show whether the sentence needs a past or present tense verb.
Then lightly shade the circle beside the verb that completes the sentence.

Past	Present			
		1. Yesterday, our class _____ on a field trip to Colonial Williamsburg.	(P) goes	(O) went
		2. Actors at Colonial Williamsburg _____ the part of colonial Americans daily.	(H) play	(K) played
		3. Carpenters laid floors, framed walls, and _____ doors.	(A) hang	(O) hung
		4. On our next visit, we'll take photos that _____ workers laying shingles on the roof of a house.	(I) show	(U) showed
		5. We _____ weavers work with wool, flax, and hemp for 30 minutes.	(S) watch	(D) watched
		6. Now, students, _____ that the brown wool is dyed using walnuts.	(M) remember	(T) remembered
		7. Shoemakers still _____ shoes in Colonial Williamsburg.	(E) craft	(R) crafted
		8. In colonial days, presses _____ laws, record books, and a gazette.	(V) print	(N) printed
		9. Today printers at Colonial Williamsburg _____ books as colonial printers did.	(O) bind	(I) bound
		10. Blacksmiths today still _____ bars of iron until they become yellow.	(D) heat	(K) heated
		11. Some of us _____ our ears when the blacksmith hammers the metal.	(T) cover	(L) covered
		12. Basketmakers _____ flexible ribbons of wood as we watched.	(C) weave	(I) wove
		13. Yesterday we _____ how nimble your fingers had to be to make baskets.	(B) notice	(N) noticed
		14. As we left, we _____ we would always remember the day we went back in time.	(F) know	(L) knew

What is a nickname for Virginia, where Colonial Williamsburg is located? To answer the question, write each shaded letter on its matching numbered line.

___ ___ ___   ___ ___ ___
11   2   7   1   14   5

___ ___ ___ ___ ___ ___ ___ ___
10   3   6   4   8   12   9   13

Choose & Do Language Arts Grids • ©The Mailbox® Books • TEC61227 • Key p. 95

Pronouns

Name _____

Date _____

Choose ____ or more activities to do.
When you finish an activity, color its number.

---

1 Copy these sentences. Underline each pronoun. Draw a line from the pronoun to the antecedent.

The bus stopped, but it pulled away quickly.

Sam began to laugh, and he couldn't stop.

The nurse winked, and then she vanished.

---

2 Complete each sentence using the pronoun that matches the subject.

THEY	IT	SHE	HE

My uncle LeQuan picked up _____.

The football field looked _____.

Mrs. Martin cooked _____.

Members of the chorus sang _____.

---

3 Rewrite each sentence. Replace each subject with one of the subject pronouns.

A spider sprinted behind the door.

A football player limped to the bench.

The waitress left the check.

The meerkats basked in the bright sun.

SHE	THEY	IT	HE

---

4 Rewrite each sentence. Replace each object with one of the object pronouns.

THEM	HIM	HER	IT

The culprit outran the officer.

I'll introduce you to my grandmother.

We are grateful to the firefighters.

There wasn't much damage to the house.

---

5 Do the practice page "Gridiron Preparations."

GO TEAM

---

6 Copy these sentences. Fill in the blanks with *I* or *me*.

Sarah and _____ shoot baskets daily.

Jay gave the books to Kim and _____.

April told Ala and _____ her plans.

Tim and _____ love to skate.

---

7 Find a story. Copy four sentences that contain *we* and four that contain *us*. Which of these pronouns is always a subject?

---

8 Think of things that belong to you and to other people. Use each possessive pronoun to write a different sentence about belongings.

mine   his   yours

theirs   its

hers   ours

---

9 Copy these sentences. Fill in the blanks with *who* or *whom*.

_____ cooked the turkey?

_____ are you expecting?

_____ should I ask?

_____ signed the declaration?

Note to the teacher: Program the student directions with the number of activities to be completed. Then copy the page and page 62 (back-to-back if desired) for each student.

Pronouns

Gridiron Preparations

Write a pronoun to complete each sentence.
Color each box that holds a possessive pronoun yellow.

me	it	ours	it	mine	their
them	his	her	she	your	us
I	its	they	we	he	his

1. The grounds crew mowed the field and used paint to mark [ ] off.

2. Sara, a photographer, checks [ ] backpack to be sure [ ] has a rain tarp.

3. A cameraperson asks, "Is this lens cover or [ ]?"

4. Members of the drill team roll up [ ] flags and place [ ] on the sidelines.

5. Mike, an announcer, tests [ ] microphone by saying, "Test, test."

6. The American flag is raised to [ ] proper height.

7. Some cheerleaders think [ ] should try that cheer just one more time.

8. "[ ] need some more towels over here," says one manager to another.

9. Jason, the mascot, thinks [ ] should practice [ ] victory dance.

10. "Don't make [ ] laugh," begged the majorettes.

11. "Mom and [ ] want two bags of popcorn," a boy says at the concession stand.

12. "If you ask [ ], we've never had a better team," said the coach.

13. Cheerleaders pull the giant banner tight so the players can burst through [ ].

14. In that moment, we're sure there's no team better than [ ].

Note to the teacher: Use with page 61.

Adjectives and Adverbs

Name _____

Date _____

Choose ____ or more activities to do.
When you finish an activity, color its number.

1 Copy the chart. Write the adverbs in the chart, sorting them by category.	**2** Complete and label three sentences, as shown, based on each incomplete sentence. Use comparative and superlative adverbs.	**3** Write an adverb that describes each verb. Then write sentences using the verb-adverb pairs.

1 Copy the chart. Write the adverbs in the chart, sorting them by category.

slowly   gently
swiftly   high
happily   around
outside   early
annually   inside

How?	When?	Where?

2 Complete and label three sentences, as shown, based on each incomplete sentence. Use comparative and superlative adverbs.

_____ runs swiftly.
_____ sings sweetly.

Simone dances beautifully.
Erin dances more beautifully than Simone. *comparative*
Diane dances most beautifully. *superlative*

3 Write an adverb that describes each verb. Then write sentences using the verb-adverb pairs.

sleep _____
yell _____
swim _____
think _____
sparkle _____

4 Make a different web for *clown*, *shark*, and *dog*. Finish each web with adjectives that describe the noun.

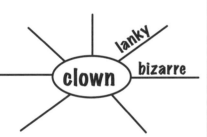

clown   lanky   bizarre

5 Do the practice page "ABCs of Description."

6 Complete and label three sentences based on each phrase. Use comparative and superlative adjectives.

wise student
intelligent decision

A fast car zoomed by.
A faster car outran his. *comparative*
The fastest car won. *superlative*

7 Find common and proper adjectives in an article. Copy four sentences that contain each type. Underline and label the adjectives.

proper
The <u>Canadian</u> coach
common
has an <u>undefeated</u>
record.

8 Write four sentences correctly using the adjective *good*. Draw arrows to show the words *good* modifies. Repeat with the adverb *well*.

Good is an adjective.

Well is an adverb.

9 Copy the chart. Complete it with appropriate adverbs.

	Comparative	Superlative
____	____	hardest
____	earlier	____
well	____	____
____	worse	____

Note to the teacher: Provide news articles for activity 7. Program the student directions with the number of activities to be completed. Then copy the page and page 64 (back-to-back if desired) for each student.

Adjectives and Adverbs

Name _____   Date _____

ABCs of Description

For each sentence below, write an adjective in the first blank and an adverb in the second blank.

Both the adjective and the adverb must begin with the circled letter.

(A) An _____ artist argued _____.

(B) Both _____ bakers began _____.

(C) The _____ counselor called _____.

(D) A _____ decorator drew _____.

(E) Each _____ executive eavesdropped _____.

(F) Four _____ fishermen forgot _____.

(G) The _____ gatekeeper guarded _____.

(H) My _____ hairdresser hummed _____.

(I) The _____ illustrator imagined _____.

(J) A _____ janitor jabbered _____.

(K) The _____ king kicked _____.

(L) The _____ lawyer leaned _____.

(M) My _____ mechanic mumbled _____.

(N) A _____ nurse nibbled _____.

(O) The _____ orthodontist organized _____.

(P) Our _____ president paused _____.

(Q) The _____ queen questioned _____.

(R) The _____ reporter replied _____.

(S) A _____ seamstress signaled _____.

(T) The _____ teacher talked _____.

(U) An _____ usher understood _____.

(V) The _____ veterinarian voyaged _____.

(W) The _____ watchman walked _____.

(X) You're excused from this one!

(Y) The _____ yachtsman yelled _____.

(Z) A _____ zookeeper zipped _____.

Choose & Do Language Arts Grids • ©The Mailbox® Books • TEC61227

Prepositions and Prepositional Phrases

Name _____

Date _____

Choose ___ or more activities to do.
When you finish an activity, color its number.

1 Cut dozens of prepositional phrases from old newspapers and magazines. Use the phrases to make a mini collage.

> throughout the day
>
> between your toes
>
> because of heavy flooding

2 Choose one of the activities below. Use eight different prepositions to write prepositional phrases that relate to that activity.

> washing a car
>
> doing a dance
>
> scoring a touchdown

3 Write three prepositional phrases to help someone identify an object in the classroom. Give the list to a friend. Can he or she guess the object?

> on the bookshelf
> beneath the leaves
> around the roots

> Is it the flowerpot?

4 Add one or more prepositional phrases to these sentences to make each one more informative. Underline each preposition and double-underline its object.

- The rock-climbing wall soars.
- Burly Bob grabs.
- Tito climbs.
- She clings.
- Miranda reaches.

5 Do the practice page "My, What a Mess!"

6 Find a recipe that has at least three prepositional phrases. Rewrite the recipe, adding a few more prepositional phrases. Mark each preposition and its object, as shown.

> **Cool the cookies**
> **on a wire rack**
> **before serving.**
>
> COOKBOOK

7 A new worker at the car wash leaves too many dirty spots. Write ten prepositional phrases that tell him places he needs to scrub.

8 Suggest a route for runners. Write seven sentences that include prepositional phrases. Mark the prepositions and objects, as shown.

> On Saturday mornings,
>
> you can jog
>
> around the parking lot
>
> at the paper mill.

9 A small class pet has escaped! Write a paragraph suggesting where to search. Include one or more prepositional phrases in each sentence.

> Before leaving the classroom, look for Mickey inside the printer.

Choose & Do Language Arts Grids • ©The Mailbox® Books • TEC61227

Note to the teacher: Provide old newspapers and magazines for activity 1 and cookbooks for activity 6. Program the student directions with the number of activities to be completed. Then copy the page and page 66 (back-to-back if desired) for each student.

65

Prepositions and Prepositional Phrases

Name _____

Date _____

My, What a Mess!

An overgrown mutt broke loose in the neighborhood. Newspapers, clotheslines, and toys were not spared.

Write about what happened when this dog got loose in your neighborhood. Use prepositional phrases in each sentence. Mark your sentences as shown below.

SOME PREPOSITIONS

about	above	according to	
across	along	around	
at	because of	before	
behind	below	beneath	
between	by	down	
during	from	in	
inside	in spite of	instead of	
into	off	on	
out	outside	over	
past	through	toward	
under	until	up	
	with	without	

With a gleam in his eye, he ran out the open door.

Note to the teacher: Use with page 65.

Phrases and Clauses

Name _____

Date _____

Choose ___ or more activities to do.
When you finish an activity, color its number.

---

1 | Choose the three dependent clauses below. Use each of them to write a sentence.

- Because she wanted to paint.
- Who eats in the cafeteria.
- The truck bounced along.
- When I see the doctor.

2 | Copy the clauses. Underline the subjects. Double-underline the predicates.

Dependent
when the coast is clear
because he isn't feeling well

Independent
She wore blue jeans.
The chef made cupcakes.

3 | Write complete sentences by combining each dependent clause with an independent clause.

Dependent
because the fire went out
when the wolves howled
who prepared our dinner

Independent
shivers went down my spine
it was your brother
we need more kindling

---

4 | Unscramble the noun phrases. Add predicates to transform them into complete sentences.

- CD the player broken
- pillow a fluffy
- my books favorite
- blanket sister's my
- mug the empty

5 | Do the practice page "Camping Tips."

6 | Copy the sentences. Put a box around the verb phrases.

- I should have helped them.
- She will be going home soon.
- It has been raining all day.
- We could have painted a picture.

---

7 | Copy the sentences. Underline the prepositional phrases. Label each one to indicate whether it tells *when* or *where*.

- The ball rolled under the bed.
- The pen was in my desk.
- On Saturday, the train will stop.
- Let's stretch before the race.

8 | Copy the sentences. Circle the appositive in each one.

- Ms. Pugh, my second-grade teacher, was there.
- Spencer College, the first one in this area, closed.
- Mr. Dennis, the mayor, will speak first.
- Aunt Lily, my dad's sister, came for a short visit.

9 | Choose a news or sports article. Underline the phrases using this key.

blue = prepositional phrase
green = verb phrase
orange = noun phrase
red = appositive

Choose & Do Language Arts Grids • ©The Mailbox® Books • TEC61227 • Key p. 96

Note to the teacher: For activity 9, provide newspaper or magazine articles. Program the student directions with the number of activities to be completed. Then copy the page and page 68 (back-to-back if desired) for each student.

Phrases and Clauses

Name _____ Date _____

Camping Tips

Underline each prepositional phrase. (Hint: three sentences don't have one.)
Then circle the letter that shows whether each boldface clause is
dependent or independent.

		dependent	independent
1.	**You need to practice pitching your tent** at home.	M	N
2.	Locate your campsite early in the day **so you will have everything ready before dark**.	O	S
3.	**Smart campers avoid staying near still water** since pesky insects prefer those locations too.	P	T
4.	**You should plan to pitch your tent** upwind of your campfire.	E	R
5.	Put your campfire at least 100 feet from your tent **so hungry bears won't visit while you snooze**.	A	B
6.	**Everyone can gather rocks** to create a fire pit.	K	C
7.	Collect some firewood **if it is permitted there**.	E	R
8.	Before setting up your tent, **you should sweep your campsite free of twigs and rocks**.	B	Y
9.	**When you see evidence of anthills**, choose another site.	O	T
10.	Because even mild storms can blow a tent away, **you will want to firmly stake yours**.	S	U
11.	**Where staking is impossible**, put a large rock in each tent corner.	R	A
12.	**Wise campers unroll their sleeping bags** on top of sleeping pads.	E	V
13.	After dark, **you will need flashlights and some extra batteries**.	S	I
14.	Purify all your drinking water **unless it comes from a clean source**.	S	C
15.	Best of all, **your family can relax and enjoy the beauty of nature**.	W	I
16.	**When it is time to leave**, douse your fire with plenty of water.	T	Y

What's the park ranger's number one camping tip?
To answer the question, write the circled letters in order on the lines.

Leave ___ ___ ___ ___ ___ ___ ___ of

___ ___ ___ ___ ___ ___ ___ ___ ___.

Complex Sentences

Name _____

Date _____

Choose ___ or more activities to do.
When you finish an activity, color its number.

after	so that	unless

so	before	if	because	where	until

while	since	when	although	as if	as

---

1 Write six complex sentences about a time in your life that you'll never forget.

   1 dependent clause
+1 independent clause
   1 complex sentence

> dependent
> While Dad parked the car,
> I bought our tickets.
> independent

2 Identify and copy the complex sentence. Revise the other two to make them complex.

- Hiking is an adventure.
- When we go camping, I help Dad with the tent.
- Campfire stories are best.

Use these subordinating conjunctions:
although   unless   as long as

3 Unscramble the following words. Use them to write six dependent clauses. Then add an independent clause to each one to make a complex sentence.

subordinating conjunctions
eeaubcs   ciens
retaf   reebof
slunse   leiwh

---

4 Underline the dependent clause. Double-underline the independent clause. Then write five more complex sentences. Mark them the same way.

> After we went to the movies, we stopped for pizza and ice cream.

5 Do the practice page "Brick by Brick."

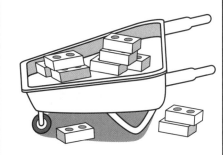

6 Copy six simple sentences from a text. Add a dependent clause to each one to make the sentence complex.

> Franklin won the contest.
>
> Since his stove was innovative, Franklin won the contest.

---

7 Find six simple sentences in a news or sports article. Change each of them to a complex sentence using related information from the article.

> The players are on strike.
>
> The players are on strike because of contract disputes.

8 Cut out an interesting photograph. Glue it on your paper. Then write five complex sentences that relate to the photo.

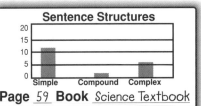

9 Select a page in a book. Examine 20 consecutive sentences to determine whether they are simple, compound, or complex. Graph and interpret your results.

> **Sentence Structures**
>
> | | | |
> |---|---|---|
> | 20 | | |
> | 15 | | |
> | 10 | | |
> | 5 | | |
> | 0 | | |
> | Simple | Compound | Complex |
>
> **Page** _59_ **Book** _Science Textbook_

Choose & Do Language Arts Grids • ©The Mailbox® Books • TEC61227 • Key p. 96

Note to the teacher: Provide newspapers or magazines for activities 7 and 8. Program the student directions with the number of activities to be completed. Then copy the page and page 70 (back-to-back if desired) for each student.

Complex Sentences

Name _____   Date _____

Brick by Brick

Part 1: Add an independent clause to complete each sentence.
Then underline the two clauses in each sentence according to the code below.

while	after	so that	unless	so

as	since	before	if	because	where	until

1. Although it was very late, _____.

2. _____ because I didn't feel well.

3. _____ since we were out of school.

4. Before I leave for school, _____.

5. Until I earn some money, _____.

6. _____ so that my parents will be proud.

Part 2: Write a dependent clause to complete each sentence.
Use a subordinating conjunction from the wall above.
Then underline the two clauses in each sentence according to the code.

> **CODE**
> red = dependent clause
> orange = independent clause

7. Mark's team won the game _____.

8. _____, I can't play today.

9. _____, my teacher always smiles.

10. Mom said I could get a new camera _____

    _____.

11. _____, we'll need to wash the car.

12. Our principal will be on television _____

    _____.

Commas

Name _____

Date _____

Choose ___ or more activities to do.
When you finish an activity, color its number.

---

1 Rewrite the following sentences. Punctuate with commas.

- I went to school gymnastics and church.
- The list included potatoes bananas and yogurt.
- I need scissors glue and a notebook.
- She has red yellow orange and blue yarn.

2 Write five sentences as though you're speaking directly to a different friend each time. Include commas.

> I heard you, Kyle, the first time.
>
> Eduarda, how do you say that in Spanish?

3 Pretend to invite a friend to five different sporting events. On each of five paper strips, write a sentence that includes the date and location (city and state) of an event.

> Here's your ticket!
>
> Let's go to see the Cowboys play on Monday, September 26, in Arlington, Texas.

4 Think of five restaurants you like. Then write a sentence for each one. In each sentence, include three or four menu items you would order.

> I'll have the house salad, clam chowder, and the rib eye steak, please.

5 Do the practice page "Pet-Lovers' Paradise."

PET SH

6 Use your social studies book to find facts about five famous Americans. Write a sentence about each person. Include an appositive.

> appositive
>
> Abraham Lincoln, <u>the 16th president of the United States</u>, was born in Kentucky.

7 Finish each of these sentences. Be sure to use a comma to separate each introductory clause (shown below) from the main sentence.

- Because my grades went down...
- When we get to my grandparents' house...
- After I make my bed...
- Since all our work is done...

8 Write a different sentence using each of these interjections. Use a comma to separate the interjection from the rest of the sentence.

WELL   OH MY
WOW   HEY
HELLO   HMMMM

9 Imagine you can read the minds of six different pets at a pet store. Write and illustrate what each animal might say. Use a comma or commas.

> "Hey," the beagle bayed, "toss me that bag of bacon treats."

Choose & Do Language Arts Grids • ©The Mailbox® Books • TEC61227 • Key p. 96

Note to the teacher: Program the student directions with the number of activities to be completed. Then copy the page and page 72 (back-to-back if desired) for each student.

Name _____ Date _____

Pet-Lovers' Paradise

Add the missing commas.
Write the sentence number beneath the matching reason for the punctuation.

1. All fish ferrets and gerbils are on sale this week.

2. Because so many dogs need homes we also feature pups from shelters.

3. Our basic grooming package includes bathing clipping and nail trimming.

4. We have adoption fairs every Sunday at our store in Sacramento California.

5. Zachary could you show this gentleman where we keep the betta food?

6. We only sell geckos at our location in Richmond Virginia.

7. I thought the guinea pig cages had already been cleaned Burt.

8. Even though all puppies are adorable not all of them make good pets for small apartments.

Use commas to separate
• items in a series
  ☐ ☐
• a city and state
  ☐ ☐
• a dependent clause from an independent clause that follows it
  ☐ ☐
• the name of a person spoken to
  ☐ ☐

9. Pepper the older black schnauzer is ready for his red bandana.

10. Our "Positively Purr-fect" sale begins Saturday February 10 at 9:00 AM.

11. Wow we are overstocked on cat food.

12. Matt whispered "Be gentle" as he passed the rabbit to the boy.

13. Ferrets are due to arrive by Tuesday September 10.

14. Oh my the chameleon is on the loose again.

15. Someone heard the cockatiel shout "Atta boy!"

16. Koi a type of Japanese fish make excellent pets for garden ponds.

Use commas
• in dates
  ☐ ☐
• to set off an interjection
  ☐ ☐
• to set off spoken words
  ☐ ☐
• to set off a phrase that explains
  ☐ ☐

Quotation Marks

Name _____

Date _____

Choose ___ or more activities to do.
When you finish an activity, color its number.

---

1 Rewrite the following sentences. Add quotation marks and other punctuation. Then write two more sentences with dialogue.

- You have practice this Saturday Mom said.

- Hey guys Peter yelled look at that airplane.

2 Choose a photo of people talking. Write their conversation. Include direct quotes that are at the beginning of a sentence and at the end of a sentence. Also include a divided quote.

3 Think of a story character that you know well. Around a drawing of him or her, write sentences that include quotes the character might say. Add responses from other characters.

Silas

"I heard you'll be selling your farm soon," Silas whispered.

"Maybe. Maybe not," his neighbor growled.

---

4 Find a section of readers' theater text or a play that you particularly enjoy. Rewrite the dialogue as it would be written in story form.

"Surely, you don't mean that!" his mother snapped.

5 Do the practice page "When the Stars Come Out."

6 Research quotes of famous Americans. Write three quotes as shown in the example. Post the quotes for others to enjoy.

In the world's first telephoned message, Alexander Graham Bell said, "Mr. Watson—come here—I want to see you."

---

7 Browse through some books written by Dr. Seuss. Copy five quotes. Phrase each quote so your readers will know which character said it.

" ~~~~~~~~~~~~~~~
~~~~~~~~~~~~~~ ,"
the Lorax shouted over the roar of the engines.

8 Ask five classmates to give their opinions about a topic. Rewrite their statements as direct quotes. Punctuate carefully.

Samuel responded, "I'd rather move to a different school than be forced to wear a goofy school uniform."

9 Recall some things teachers repeatedly say or reminders you hear on the school announcements. Write five of them as direct quotes.

"Students, remember there is no school tomorrow," our principal said, just before a loud cheer erupted. Yay!

Choose & Do Language Arts Grids • ©The Mailbox® Books • TEC61227 • Key p. 96

Note to the teacher: Program the student directions with the number of activities to be completed. Then copy the page and page 74 (back-to-back if desired) for each student.

Quotation Marks

Name _____ Date _____

When the Stars Come Out

Underline the exact words spoken.
Add quotation marks where they belong.

⭐1	Crowds chanted, Let us in! as they waited for the doors to open.	⭐9	Oh, look! a young girl shouted. There's Babette!
⭐2	Then someone shouted, There's a limo headed this way!	⭐10	As cameras clicked, Babette smiled and asked, How's this?
⭐3	Step back, the usher said. Please remain behind the velvet ropes.	⭐11	Isn't this dress divine? the diva crooned.
⭐4	A chauffeur opened the door and warned, Watch your step, sir.	⭐12	She admitted, It was designed by Sara Chang.
⭐5	Heartthrob Harry emerged saying, Would you look at this crowd?	⭐13	Then she revealed her new pocket pooch, saying, Isn't it the cutest thing?
⭐6	He whispered, Where did all these people come from, dude?	⭐14	Girls lining the red carpet chimed, Awwww!
⭐7	How's my hair? he asked as he checked his reflection.	⭐15	A bodyguard motioned for the couple to move on, saying, It's almost showtime.
⭐8	Check to see if I have some spinach in my teeth, please, he begged.	⭐16	Whisking Babette inside, Harry shouted to the crowd, You're going to love the show!

Choose & Do Language Arts Grids • ©The Mailbox® Books • TEC61227 • Key p. 96

Note to the teacher: Use with page 73.

Writing Paragraphs

Name _____

Date _____

Choose ___ or more activities to do.
When you finish an activity, color its number.

1 Rearrange these sentences to make a well-organized paragraph. Write it. • In my last class, science, I got an A on my test. • Yesterday, I had the best day ever! • Then the cafeteria served my favorite lunch. • If only every day could be that great. • During morning announcements, I was named Citizen of the Week.	**2** Write a paragraph. Explain how to do one of the following tasks: wrap a package make a banana split throw a football tie a shoe 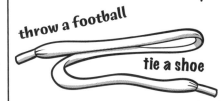	**3** Finish this paragraph about a time you were injured. Use the transition words given. Everything was fine, but then it happened. First, Next, Then Finally, 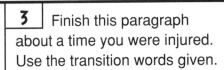
4 Complete the paragraph below. Add descriptive details that support the topic sentence. **Topic sentence:** Our team works really hard. • • • **Conclusion:** We are so well prepared, we are sure to win.	**5** Do the practice page "Penciling In a Plan." 	**6** Write a paragraph summarizing a funny story a relative told you. Draw a picture of your relative telling the story. HA! HA! HA!
7 Write a paragraph using the details below. Add a topic sentence and conclusion that fit well with the details provided. Topic sentence: _____ • In middle school, you get to have lots of different teachers. • More homework is assigned. • Most middle school students get to have a locker. Concluding sentence: _____	**8** Write a paragraph on one of the topics below. Use colored pencils to write your topic sentence and conclusion in red. Write the details in blue. • the best sporting event I've ever seen • the nicest thing anyone has done for me • the hardest thing I've ever had to do	**9** Remember a time you cooked something. Complete a web like the one shown. Write a paragraph with the web's details. 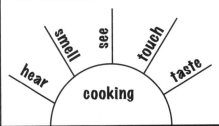

Choose & Do Language Arts Grids • ©The Mailbox® Books • TEC61227 • Key p. 96

Note to the teacher: Program the student directions with the number of activities to be completed. Then copy the page and page 76 (back-to-back if desired) for each student.

75

Name _____

Date _____

Writing Paragraphs

Penciling In a Plan

Use this organizer to plan three paragraphs.

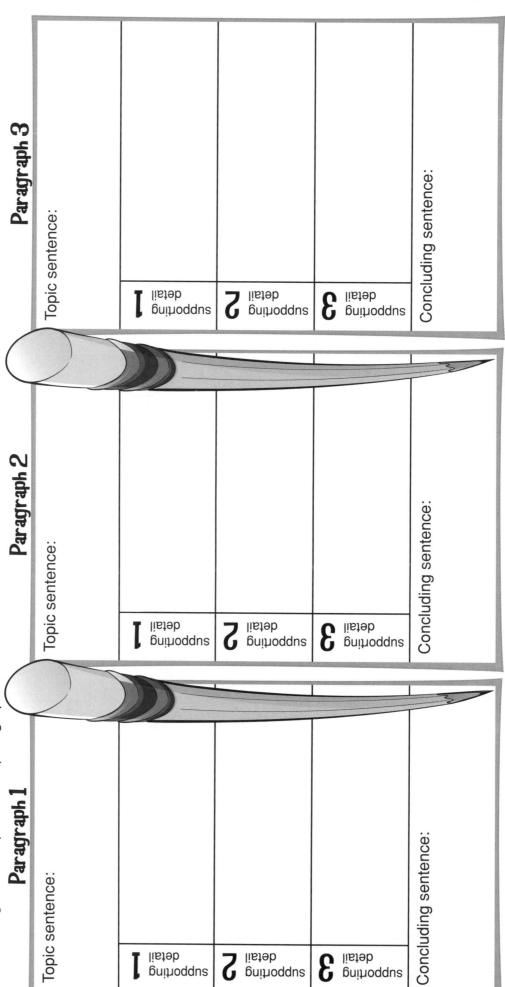

Paragraph 1

Topic sentence:

supporting detail 1

supporting detail 2

supporting detail 3

Concluding sentence:

Paragraph 2

Topic sentence:

supporting detail 1

supporting detail 2

supporting detail 3

Concluding sentence:

Paragraph 3

Topic sentence:

supporting detail 1

supporting detail 2

supporting detail 3

Concluding sentence:

Choose & Do Language Arts Grids • ©The Mailbox® Books • TEC61227

Note to the teacher: Use with page 75.

Writing Dialogue

Name _____

Date _____

Choose ____ or more activities to do.
When you finish an activity, color its number.

1 Add quotation marks and commas to the following. Write the sentences. • **You have practice this Saturday Mom said.** • **Hey, guys Peter yelled Look at that plane!** • **As he scratched his head, Jake mumbled I'm not sure.**	**2** Choose a character and complete a web like the one shown. Then write five lines of dialogue that this person might say. • **a truck driver** • **a cheerleader** • **a basketball player** 	**3** For each of these situations, list three words a writer could use instead of *said* when writing dialogue. **"Oh my," the lady ~~said~~.** • frustrated by a flat tire • sad over the loss of a pet • excited to have made the team • tired after practice
4 Write a conversation between two characters. Use a different-color pencil for each character's dialogue.  "I don't want to go," the man barked. She inquired, "Why not?"	**5** Do the practice page "Yakety-Yak." YAKETY YAK!	**6** Copy the sentence below five times, changing the underlined verb each time. Explain how changing the verb changes the meaning of the sentence. "I can't believe it," Erica <u>mumbled</u>.
7 The underlined words are *dialogue tags*. Write two different dialogue tags for each letter below. "You lied!" Mary <u>hissed</u>. "I am not afraid" Cory <u>replied</u>. W I T B S P R M	**8** Write a conversation you'd love to have with the person you most admire. I admire you...	**9** Reread a section from a play or readers' theater. Rewrite it as dialogue. Use a variety of dialogue tags. Indent each time a different speaker starts speaking. **Readers' Theater**

Choose & Do Language Arts Grids • ©The Mailbox® Books • TEC61227 • Key p. 96

Note to the teacher: Provide plays or readers' theater scripts for activity 9. Program the student directions with the number of activities to be completed. Then copy the page and page 78 (back-to-back if desired) for each student.

77

Writing Dialogue

Name _____ Date _____

Sometimes mention what the character does during the conversation.

nodded head
shuffled feet
wrung hands
wiped away tears
looked nervously around
cleared throat
clenched fist
adjusted cap
took a step closer
smiled
shrugged

Instead of said, choose:

replied	questioned
nagged	confessed
hissed	barked
sighed	muttered
admitted	laughed
sobbed	snarled
agreed	

Characters

police officer and driver	wizard and apprentice
coach and player	principal and student
child and grandparent	guide and tourist
child and game store clerk	dog obedience trainer and dog owner

Yakety-Yak

Choose a pair of characters from the pocket.
Use the tips in the pocket.
Write the characters' conversation.

Note to the teacher: Use with page 77.

Writing Tasks

Name _____

Date _____

Choose ____ or more activities to do.
When you finish an activity, color its number.

1 Write a story about bubble gum trouble. Display it alongside a picture you draw of your bubble gum catastrophe.

It burst all over my face.

It made a huge BANG!

It won't come off my teeth.

2 Analyze a story you previously wrote. Rate it on each of the traits below. List three revisions that will improve it.

What's your score?					
great beginning	I	2	3	4	5
sensory details	I	2	3	4	5
elaboration	I	2	3	4	5
vivid verbs	I	2	3	4	5
thoughtful ending	I	2	3	4	5

3 Write to describe a radical new hairstyle that's all the rage. Use at least three kinds of figurative language. Post a drawing of the hairstyle with your description.

SIMILE
METAPHOR
HYPERBOLE
ONOMATOPOEIA
PERSONIFICATION

4 The unimaginable has happened. Choose one of the fiascos below. Write a story about it. Emphasize what you see, hear, and feel.

- The tub is overflowing and won't stop.
- Your prank landed you in the principal's office.
- You're breaking out in purple spots.

5 Do the practice page "Gizmos and Gadgets."

6 Pretend you just won a million dollars. In a paragraph, describe how you reacted to the news.

7 A Martian is staying with you a while. Some things in your house frighten it. Explain to it precisely how one of these things is used and why we need it.

toaster
vacuum cleaner
paper shredder
hair dryer

8 Write a persuasive letter giving several good reasons why one of these animals should be your pet. Predict the main objection. Explain why it won't be a problem.

python   **elephant**

iguana   **tiger**

9 Write a step-by-step description of a common task. Be exact in describing what to do. Have a friend read your instructions and ask you questions about them.

- **how to draw a happy face**
- **how to make a paper airplane**
- **how to bathe a dog**

Choose & Do Language Arts Grids • ©The Mailbox® Books • TEC61227

Note to the teacher: Program the student directions with the number of activities to be completed. Then copy the page and page 80 (back-to-back if desired) for each student.

79

Name _____ Date _____

Gizmos and Gadgets

Some things in your house confuse a Martian friend!
Choose an appliance. Organize your thoughts here.
Then write to explain to your friend how to operate the appliance.

GIZMO OR GADGET: _____

PURPOSE: _____

How does it sound when it's working?	How does it look?	How does it feel when it's working?	What does it smell like?
It sounds as _____ as a _____.	It looks like a _____ about to _____.	It's as _____ as a _____ _____.	It smells as _____ as a _____.

How do you operate it?

1. _____
_____

2. _____
_____

3. _____
_____

4. _____
_____

5. _____
_____

Choose & Do Language Arts Grids • ©The Mailbox® Books • TEC61227

Writing Tasks

Name _____

Date _____

Choose ___ or more activities to do.
When you finish an activity, color its number.

Family

1 Write and illustrate an imaginative story that explains how an unusual-looking animal got its looks.

**how the camel got its hump
how the giraffe got a long neck
how the rhinoceros got its horn**

2 Analyze a story you wrote. Circle the nouns and underline the verbs. Revise some nouns to be more specific. Revise some verbs to be more vivid.

reporter   hustled
The (man) walked.

3 Pretend you're a pet up for adoption. Write a letter describing your finer qualities and explaining the kind of home you need. Tell what kinds of adventures you look forward to.

Yours truly,
Patches

4 Choose a photograph of a person. Pretend you witnessed that person running from a crime scene. Write a clear description of the person for the police report.

facial features and expressions

clothing   BODY (TYPE)

movements   sounds

5 Do the practice page "My Remarkable Relative."

6 Research an American landmark. Write a paragraph that answers these questions: Who? What? Where? When? Why?

7 Write a description of your classroom. Be so specific that a person visiting your school would be able to identify it just from your description. (Don't include your room number or teacher's name!)

8 Write a persuasive letter to your principal. Explain why your school mascot must be changed and what it should become. Predict the main objection and explain why it's not a problem.

Go Hawks!

9 Write a step-by-step description of how to do one of the tasks below. Be exact in describing what to do.

• how to make a bed
• how to make toast
• how to be a good friend

Choose & Do Language Arts Grids • ©The Mailbox® Books • TEC61227

Note to the teacher: Provide old magazines for activity 4. Program the student directions with the number of activities to be completed. Then copy the page and page 82 (back-to-back if desired) for each student.

81

Writing Tasks

Name _____   Date _____

My Remarkable Relative

Choose a relative to interview. Make notes on this page.
Then write a report about that person using these notes.

My remarkable relative's name: _____

What was this person known for as a child?	What is this person known for as an adult?
Where did this person like to be as a child?	Where does this person like to be as an adult?
Who were the important people in this person's childhood?	Who are the important people in this person's life now?
What is a favorite childhood memory?	What is a favorite memory from adulthood?

On your own, determine a character trait of this person.

Character Trait   What evidence is there of this trait?

Letters, Invitations, and Notes

Name _____

Date _____

Choose ___ or more activities to do.
When you finish an activity, color its number.

1	Write a friendly letter to a new student. Explain three important things about your school. Give your new pal some advice.

WELCOME
to Our
Cool School!

2	Label a page as shown. Describe how all the parts of friendly and business letters compare.

Friendly Letter	Both	Business Letter
heading starts at center	heading: sender's address and date	heading starts at left
no inside address		has an inside address

3	Write a friendly letter to someone who's having trouble with a video game. Explain three things she or he can do to win.

4	A business letter explains a problem or a need or makes a request. List five situations that might require you to write a business letter.

Can you help us?

5	Do the practice page "Letter-Perfect."

6	On index cards, write invitations to three different events your school may have this year. Decorate each one with festive drawings.

You are invited to our Fall Festival. Meet us on the school playground Saturday, October 23, at 5:00 PM. We'll have games, a cake walk, face painting, and fun prizes. There will be piping hot pizza and apple cider too. Bring your family and friends. Everyone is invited.

7	Think of someone who does a lot for children at your school. Write and illustrate a thank-you note for that person.

Thank You

8	Write a business letter to your school's parent-teacher association. Ask that they buy something from this list. Explain how it would help kids.

- **playground equipment**
- **technology equipment**
- **specific books**

9	Write a friendly letter to your teacher for one of the following reasons.

- Explain a recent low grade and how you'll avoid another one.
- Tell about your favorite book and ask for more books like it.

Choose & Do Language Arts Grids • ©The Mailbox® Books • TEC61227 • Key p. 96

Note to the teacher: Supply index cards and sample invitations for activity 6 and sample thank-you notes for activity 7. Program the student directions with the number of activities to be completed. Then copy the page and page 84 (back-to-back, if desired) for each student.

83

Name _____

Date _____

Friendly and Business Letters

Letter-Perfect

Study both examples.

Then choose one of the writing options. Write your letter on your own paper.

Friendly Letter Format

4405 Maple Street
Yakima, Washington 98901
March 10, 2013

Dear Bryce,

When we moved here, I wasn't sure I would like Meadowview School. That was before I knew all that goes on here. For one thing, you will like our teachers. All of them are good and some of them are funny. They're the best!

We have special clubs here too. One time I was in the karate club. I wish you could have seen the coach break a board with his hand. I'm looking forward to trying other clubs, like the school newspaper and cooking club.

The best part of being here is making tons of friends. I know you will feel at home here soon. I'll see you on the playground!

Your classmate,
Carlos Miles

Business Letter Format

5288 Mill Street
Atlanta, GA 30304
March 10, 2013

Mr. Harold Dixon
Logan Lumber Yard
PO Box 29
Macon, GA 31210

Dear Mr. Dixon:

Parents and kids are working on a plan for an outdoor classroom at Harris Elementary School. Science teachers say we will discover a lot about plants and insects outside. Other teachers say that nature can inspire poetry and stories.

We need wood to make benches for this project. Would your company donate some lumber? We also need carpenters to teach us how to build furniture and painters to show us how to protect the wood from the weather. If you can help, please call our school to let us know.

Thank you for considering this. We appreciate any help you can offer.

Sincerely,
Cindy Martin
Cindy Martin

heading

inside address

greeting

body

closing

signature

Writing options:
- Write a friendly letter to a new student about what makes your school special.
- Write a business letter to Mr. Dixon of the Logan Lumber Yard. Ask him to be a speaker at your class's Career Day.

Choose & Do Language Arts Grids • ©The Mailbox® Books • TEC61227

Note to the teacher: Use with page 83.

Dictionary and Thesaurus Skills

Name _____

Date _____

Choose ___ or more activities to do.
When you finish an activity, color its number.

1 Copy the web. Finish it with words from a thesaurus that have the same meaning or similar meanings. Create another web for *good*. 	**2** List the words below in alphabetical order. Beside each word, write the dictionary page that it appears on. Check the order of the page numbers to see if your list was ordered correctly. skateboard ramp jump helmet exhilaration balance accelerate	**3** Copy the words below. Locate each one in a dictionary. Write the corresponding guide words for each word. velocity agility nimble safety equipment physical ramp flexibility air gravity
4 Copy each sentence. Rewrite it three different ways, changing the underlined words with the help of a thesaurus. • <u>Friends</u> <u>like</u> to play <u>games</u> together. • <u>Carry</u> the <u>bag</u> inside.	**5** Do the practice page "Sidewalk Surfing." 	**6** Make a chart as shown. Use a dictionary to complete the chart for each of these words. wheel sport popular deck modern competition helmet freestyle rail traction trucks axle | Word	Part of Speech	Language of Origin	Number of Meanings
---	---	---	---
7 Make a small poster proclaiming the wonders of a word of your choice. Use a dictionary and thesaurus. Write about uses of this word and its relatives. 	**8** Copy a paragraph from a chapter book, skipping lines. Underline ten action verbs. Use a thesaurus to find more vivid word choices for the marked words. Revise the paragraph.	**9** Alphabetize and number the words below. Write the dictionary guide words for each even-numbered word. Write the part(s) of speech for the remaining words. globe thesaurus index map atlas almanac glossary copyright bibliography newspaper research schedule

Note to the teacher: Program the student directions with the number of activities to be completed. Then copy the page and page 86 (back-to-back if desired) for each student.

Name _____   Date _____

Sidewalk Surfing

Look at the boldfaced word in each sentence.
Write the letter of the matching guide word pair in each blank.

_____ 1. Skateboarding started because surfers wanted to **surf** when the waves were flat.

_____ 2. The first skateboarders used boards with roller **skate** wheels attached.

_____ 3. Some people called it **sidewalk** surfing.

_____ 4. Skateboarders tried surfing-style **maneuvers**.

_____ 5. Surfboard companies began to **manufacture** skateboards that looked like small surfboards.

_____ 6. A new **magazine** helped make the sport popular across the nation.

_____ 7. Developers improved the **wheel** design of skateboards.

_____ 8. The new wheels got better **traction** than the older, metal ones did.

_____ 9. Companies then started to make new axles, called **trucks**, which improved maneuverability.

_____ 10. The trend became to make the skateboard decks up to ten inches **wide**.

_____ 11. Common skateboards were made of **maple** plywood.

_____ 12. Others were made of composites and different types of **metal**.

_____ 13. Because the new skateboards handled better, people came up with new **tricks**.

_____ 14. They even used them to skate the **walls** of empty swimming pools.

a. tract–traffic	**h**. manse–manuscript
b. many–march	**i**. tributary–tricolor
c. walk–wane	**j**. maddening–magisterial
d. sidesplitting–sign	**k**. whaleboat–wheelbase
e. mandible–mania	**l**. troposphere–trudge
f. whopper–wieldy	**m**. sixty–sketchy
g. supposition–surface	**n**. mesosphere–metallic

Choosing the Right References

Name _____

Date _____

Choose ___ or more activities to do.
When you finish an activity, color its number.

| Almanac |
| Dictionary |
| ENCYCLOPEDIA |
| World Atlas |

---

1 Compare three different dictionaries. List their similarities and differences. Write a note to your classmates explaining which is the best for you and why.

2 Examine two different atlases. List their similarities and differences. Write an explanation about which you prefer.

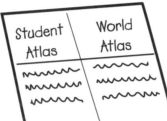

Student Atlas | World Atlas

3 Examine an almanac. List six of the most interesting things it contains. Then list six specific entries you might use in the future for schoolwork.

Who knew?

---

4 Label your paper as shown. Then look up *England* in each source. Write the kinds of things each reference reveals about England.

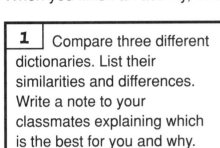

England			
dictionary	encyclopedia	atlas	almanac

5 Do the practice page "Tools of the Grade."

6 Complete a Venn diagram by listing the helpful tools (such as a map or a meaning) each reference provides for the term *continent*.

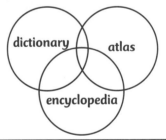

dictionary   atlas   encyclopedia

---

7 Pretend you are one of the references below. Apply for a job in a social studies class. Explain in writing what a hard worker you are and exactly how you'll help if you get the chance.

dictionary
atlas
almanac
encyclopedia

8 Sketch a billboard that advertises a specific reference, such as a dictionary or an atlas.

ONLINE DICTIONARY

Where word wisdom is only a click away!

ONLINE DICTIONARY

9 Write a song or poem explaining when to use each of the references below. Share it with classmates.

dictionary   atlas
almanac   thesaurus
encyclopedia

Choose & Do Language Arts Grids • ©The Mailbox® Books • TEC61227

Note to the teacher: Provide access to several different dictionaries, encyclopedias, almanacs, thesauruses, and atlases. Program the student directions with the number of activities to be completed. Then copy the page and page 88 (back-to-back if desired) for each student.

Choosing the Right References

Name _____   Date _____

Tools of the Grade

Read each statement.
Shade the space that shows the best
resource to use.

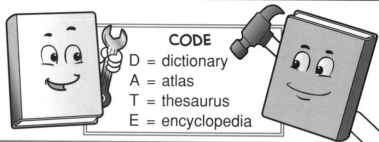

CODE
D = dictionary
A = atlas
T = thesaurus
E = encyclopedia

1.	Zachary wonders how many of our 50 states border the Pacific Ocean.	D	A	T	E
2.	Anaya is writing a report. She thinks she has overused the word *dog*.	D	A	T	E
3.	Evan is preparing for the science fair, and he wants to know how to pronounce *inquiry*.	D	A	T	E
4.	Nicholas needs to know whether the Galapagos Islands are closer to the equator than the Hawaiian Islands are.	D	A	T	E
5.	Amelia is adding dialogue to her stories. She knows she can't use *said* repeatedly.	D	A	T	E
6.	Nate is going to do a report on the Wampanoag natives of New England.	D	A	T	E
7.	Owen thinks that *quick* and *rapid* are synonyms.	D	A	T	E
8.	Reagan is wondering whether *vacant* is an adjective or a verb.	D	A	T	E
9.	When Daniel rereads his story, he notices he used the word *run* over and over.	D	A	T	E
10.	Samuel thinks that *accept* and *except* mean the same thing.	D	A	T	E
11.	Miranda wants to know what constellations are and the history behind their names.	D	A	T	E
12.	Abby wants to know if Brazil is a country on the east coast of South America.	D	A	T	E
13.	Jay wants to know whether Germany shares a border with France.	D	A	T	E
14.	Amanda's mom says Amanda is a perfectionist. She's not completely sure what that is.	D	A	T	E
15.	Carol wonders if *quiet* is a one-syllable word.	D	A	T	E
16.	Brian wonders how to plant tulip bulbs and when they will bloom.	D	A	T	E
17.	Griffin is not sure if the *a* in *water* is a short *a* sound.	D	A	T	E
18.	Kennedy wonders how the Caldecott Award got its name.	D	A	T	E

Choose & Do Language Arts Grids • ©The Mailbox® Books • TEC61227 • Key p. 96

Name _____

Date _____

Choose ___ or more activities to do.
When you finish an activity, color its number.

1	2	3
4	5 	6
7	8	9

Choose & Do Language Arts Grids • ©The Mailbox® Books • TEC61227

Note to the teacher: Make a copy of this page. Program the top with a book title or skill and program the student directions with the number of activities to be completed. Write a different activity in each grid space and make a class supply.

Page 5

Answers for 3 and 6–9 will vary.

1. <u>It's</u> a bouncing baby boy.
   <u>It's</u> about time.
   <u>Its</u> buttons were gone.
   <u>It's</u> now or never.

2. breath
   mumble under your <u>breath</u>
   <u>breath</u> of fresh air
   catch your <u>breath</u>

   breathe
   <u>breathe</u> new life into
   <u>breathe</u> deeply

4. lose
   nothing to <u>lose</u>
   <u>lose</u> sleep
   <u>lose</u> his way

   loose
   a <u>loose</u> tooth
   wear your hair <u>loose</u>
   a <u>loose</u> plank

Page 6

1. <u>It's</u> almost time for our science exam.
2. The projector just blew <u>its</u> bulb.
3. No homework? Don't hold your <u>breath</u>.
4. When he sees this grade, he will <u>breathe</u> a sigh of relief.
5. The pencil <u>lead</u> always breaks!
6. Several factors <u>led</u> to his suspension.
7. If you <u>lose</u> your study guide, you will regret it.
8. The leg of my desk wiggles because it's <u>loose</u>.
9. Because it contains <u>personal</u> information, the envelope is sealed.
10. School <u>personnel</u> frown upon chewing gum at school.
11. The two runners were in a <u>duel</u> for first place.
12. There are <u>dual</u> methods for contacting the principal.
13. When you write a report, you must <u>cite</u> your sources.
14. The <u>site</u> for our school garden has been staked off.
15. Everyone <u>except</u> Trevor has returned his form on time.
16. She will <u>accept</u> my excuse about what happened.
17. Weather can really <u>affect</u> my mood.
18. Today's sunshine had a good <u>effect</u> on my mood.

Page 7

Answers for 2–4 and 6–8 will vary.

1.
brave	braved	braving
zone	zoned	zoning
save	saved	saving
spike	spiked	spiking
mute	muted	muting
smile	smiled	smiling
pave	paved	paving
time	timed	timing
quake	quaked	quaking

9. I <u>carried</u> my cell phone as I <u>walked</u> to your house. Joe <u>phoned</u> and <u>asked</u> if I was <u>planning</u> on <u>staying</u> and <u>playing</u> with you. I <u>invited</u> him to join us. He is <u>racing</u> here now. I <u>tried</u> to call you, but your phone was busy.

Page 8

Answers will vary.

<u>Praying</u> mantises are found in the United States. They can also be <u>located</u> in tropical places around the world. <u>Spotting</u> one is not easy. Mantises are very good at <u>blending</u> in with the plants they are <u>resting</u> on. Mantises come in all sizes, <u>ranging</u> from one centimeter long to six inches long.

Mantises are known for <u>posing</u> with their arms <u>propped</u> up. This pose makes them look as though they are praying. Motionless, they seem to be <u>scanning</u> the area with their huge eyes. These eyes are <u>mounted</u> on a triangular head. This head turns 180 degrees for <u>detecting</u> prey. When an insect comes within <u>striking</u> distance, the mantis snatches it with its <u>spiked</u> forelegs. Then the praying mantis uses its mouth parts to start <u>cutting</u> and <u>tearing</u> through the insect's body.

Sometimes, however, this predator can become prey. Male praying mantises fly at night. They are <u>attracted</u> to lights. Bats use sound waves that help in <u>locating</u> insects like mantises. A praying mantis only has one ear. It uses its ear as a tool for <u>hearing</u> and <u>dodging</u> a bat attack. If a <u>flying</u> mantis senses a mild threat from a bat, it begins slowly <u>turning</u>. But if it senses a deadly threat, it begins <u>twirling</u> and <u>diving</u> toward the ground, <u>saving</u> itself from the clutches of the bat.

Page 14

Main idea: A chef does many different jobs
Detail 1: He plans menus.
Detail 2: He orders food and supplies.
Detail 3: He cooks and teaches others to cook.
Detail 4: He guides the work in the kitchen.

Main idea: Chefs work in many locations.
Detail 1: Some work in restaurants.
Detail 2: Some work in hospitals and other health-care locations.
Detail 3: Some work in hotels, lodges, resorts, or aboard cruise ships.
Detail 4: Some prepare food for weddings and parties.

Page 15

Answers for 2–4 and 6–9 will vary.

1.
Cause	Effect
joke	laughter
fall	bruise
grief	tears
dust	sneeze
alarm	awake

Students' word pairs will vary.

Page 16

Cause	Effect
Baby spiders must be able to spin their own silk.	Baby spiders stay inside their egg sacs for a while.
Spiderlings shed their exoskeletons and grow new ones.	This allows them to grow larger.
Spiderwebs are hard to see.	An insect may not see a web and fly right into it.
Spiders make webs with strands of sticky silk.	A trapped insect only gets more stuck as it struggles.
Spiders can feel trapped insects tugging on their webs.	This lets them know it's time to eat.
Spiders know where the sticky parts of their webs are.	They don't get stuck in their own webs.
Sometimes spiders aren't ready to eat their prey.	They make a silk case around it and put it in a safe place for later.
Spiders eat many, many insects.	Spiders can help farmers get rid of insect pests.
Spiders often need to make quick escapes.	They descend on silk threads that can be quickly climbed.
Small spiders release silk threads and get carried away on breezes.	They can travel great distances, even out to sea.

Page 18

Facts: 1, 4, 5, 7, 8, 10, 12, 14, 15, 17
Opinions:
2. Americans spend <u>too much</u> of their food budget on pizza.
3. The <u>best</u> pizza on the planet is made in Nome, Alaska.
6. A <u>good</u> tip for a pizza delivery driver is two dollars.
9. Hand-tossed crust has <u>better</u> flavor than rolled crust.
11. It's <u>terrible</u> to put gourmet toppings like caviar on pizza.
13. The <u>worst</u> pizza topping of all time is squid.
16. Hawaiian pizza, with its golden pineapple chunks, is a <u>wonderful</u> choice.
18. Fried egg pizzas will <u>never</u> be popular in the United States.

Page 19

Answers for 2–4 and 6–9 will vary.

1. Answers will vary.
   A girl entered a piano competition. Even though she was nervous, all her practice paid off. She won.

Page 20

1. Why are robots needed?
2. What kinds of jobs can robots do?
3. How does a robot know what to do?

Summaries will vary.

Page 27

Answers will vary for 1–4, 8, and 9.

6. Order will vary.
eight, ate
steak, stake
heel, heal
real, reel
gait, gate
break, brake
steal, steel

7. four, for
sore, soar
peak, peek
weak, week

Sentences will vary.

Page 28

1. N, presence
2. O, pause
3. T, Which
4. H, hour
5. I, piece
6. N, knead
7. G, role
8. J, sew
9. U, ceiling
10. S, whether
11. T, allowed
12. W, cellar
13. A, hire
14. V, capital
15. E, bale
16. D, flee

<u>NOTHING</u>. It <u>JUST WAVED</u>.

Page 29

Answers for 6–9 will vary.

1. Answers will vary.
Don't count your chickens before they hatch: Wait for a good thing to happen before being certain that it will.
Don't put all your eggs in one basket: Don't risk everything by counting on one plan to be successful.
You're no spring chicken: You're not young anymore.

2. The idiom that doesn't fit is "give one's right arm," which means to give something of great value. The other idioms relate to a person who is not in a good position either through sickness, exhaustion, lack of necessities, or being overwhelmed.
under the weather = feeling sick
run out of steam = being tired or exhausted
up a creek without a paddle = not having what you need to be successful
bite off more than you can chew = taking on too much to do

3. Sentences will vary.

Happy	**Unhappy**
crack me up	hot under the collar
on cloud nine	a chip on your shoulder
as pleased as punch	fit to be tied
	drive her up the wall
	get up on the wrong side of the bed

4. Answers will vary.
raining cats and dogs: a heavy downpour of rain
the apple of my eye: special
when pigs fly: that's impossible
lost his head: started acting irrationally

Page 30

1. c
2. j
3. k
4. d
5. e
6. m
7. n
8. f
9. g
10. h
11. l
12. a
13. b
14. i

Page 32

Tickets for 1, 3, 11, 13, 15, and 18 should be colored yellow.

1. Jeremy's brain was a <u>battlefield</u>. Should he ride or not?
2. My sister, on the other hand, got a place in line <u>as quick as a wink</u>.
3. "<u>This ride is a rocket</u>. You'll love it!" I tried to reassure Jeremy.
4. As we were climbing that first hill, my sister was <u>shaking like a leaf</u>.
5. She <u>quivered like a bowl of gelatin</u> as she grabbed the safety bar.
6. I have to admit, my heart was also <u>racing like a rabbit</u>!
7. The noise was <u>as loud as a locomotive</u> when we went around curves.
8. At the highest point, my cousin, Harry, turned <u>as white as a sheet</u>.
9. Tyrell revealed that Mom <u>cried like a baby</u> until the very end.
10. She claimed the log flume was <u>as high as Mount Everest</u>.
11. Oddly, the <u>hyena</u> in the seat behind me couldn't stop laughing.
12. We <u>shot forward like a bullet</u> after teetering for a second at the very top.
13. When we finally leveled out, the <u>noise around us was an avalanche</u>.
14. All I could hear was people <u>cackling like hens</u> as we came to a sudden halt.
15. Where's a mirror? I have to see this sopping wet <u>haystack</u> on my head.
16. Look at Melissa! She's <u>as wet as a fish</u>.
17. Hey! How did Harry manage to stay <u>as dry as toast</u>?
18. That <u>log ride was a pleasure cruise</u>. Let's go again!

<u>A TOWEL</u>

Page 33

Answers for 1–4, 6, 8, and 9 will vary.

7. Answers will vary.

hand	part of a human arm	a pointer on a dial	a skilled person
land	surface of the earth	come to rest in a place	real estate
fan	to spread like a fan	an admirer	something that makes a current of air
ground	surface of the earth	coffee beans after brewing	a reason
tackle	equipment for an activity	to grapple with	the act of tackling
pass	a permit or ticket	low place in mountains	transfer a ball to a teammate

Page 34

1. t
2. h
3. o
4. c
5. s
6. l
7. p
8. i
9. e
10. k

<u>hot pickles</u>

Page 35

Answers for 4 and 7–9 will vary.

1. calm, nervous; antonyms
bumpy, rough; synonyms
red, scarlet; synonyms
laugh, cry; antonyms
flower, bloom; synonyms
light, dark; antonyms
play, work; antonyms
speak, talk; synonyms

2. Answers will vary.
good: fine, superior, excellent, wonderful, great
big: bulky, goodly, grand, great, husky, largish, sizable, voluminous
small: bitty, little, miniature, puny, teensy, tiny, wee
run: dash, gallop, jog, scamper, sprint, trot
said: remarked, spoke, stated, talked, told, uttered
wonder: ponder, marvel, speculate, puzzle over

3. Answers will vary.
joy: sorrow, sadness, grief, heartbreak, anguish, woe, misery, unhappiness, ill-being
filthy: clean, spotless, immaculate, spick-and-span, stainless, unsoiled
timid: bold, brave, courageous, daring, adventurous, gutsy
enemy: friend, comrade, pal, buddy, confidant, mate, ally, partner
ordinary: extraordinary, odd, strange, unusual, exceptional, rare
lazy: active, industrious, energetic, ambitious, lively, peppy, perky, zippy

6.
Synonyms	Antonyms
tasty, delicious	depart, arrive
quick, speedy	high, low
sweet, sugary	brave, cowardly
shout, yell	nervous, calm

Page 36

	antonyms	synonyms	neither
1. sow, harvest	G	S	H
2. sprout, germinate	T	G	P
3. moist, dry	C	E	T
4. forecast, predict	Y	A	S
5. sow, plant	F	R	N
6. fungus, fertilize	S	O	P
7. ripen, mature	C	V	W
8. harvest, gather	Q	E	Z
9. shovel, hoe	M	W	V
10. cultivate, plow	E	N	O
11. shallow, deep	H	V	U
12. transplant, move	I	H	G
13. dig, weeds	L	C	S
14. site, location	A	O	M
15. foliage, vegetation	U	S	R
16. trim, prune	B	E	C

garden hose

Page 37

Answers for 1, 3, 4, 6, and 9 will vary.

2. Sentences and definitions will vary.

I work for an international company.
Inter- means between or among.

Relax and don't overdo it.
Over- means excessively.

That singer is extraordinary!
Extra- means beyond the scope of.

Your room is disorganized.
Dis- means the absence of something.

7. director   borrower   narrator
   governor   surveyor   examiner
   counselor   reporter   illustrator
   believer   inventor   visitor

8. election
   subtraction
   attraction
   collection
   instruction
   destruction
   protection
   connection
   prediction
   Each word is a noun.

Page 38

Words With Prefixes
transcribe
postseason
autograph
hemisphere
periscope
cohabit
equidistant

Words With Prefixes and Suffixes
semiconductor
decoder
discontentment
reactor
undeniably
insensitive

Words With Suffixes
kingdom
teacher
homeless
violinist
capability
assistance
poetic

Page 40

astro   *geo*
astronomy   geometry
astronaut   geographic
astrophysics   geology

bio   *photo*
biologist   photograph
biome   photocopy
biography   photosynthesis

Sentences will vary.

Page 43

1. *Small* is to *tiny* as *huge* is to giant.
   Near is to *close* as *far* is to distant.
   Tasty is to *delicious* as *hungry* is to starving.
   Nervous is to *tense* as *calm* is to peaceful.

2. slim : fat :: thin : wide
   dark : light :: night : day
   smooth : rough :: straight : curved
   hot : cold :: melt : freeze

3. Answers will vary.
   Kittens are to cats as puppies are to dogs.
      This analogy relates offspring to the matching adult animal.
   Bees are to honey as cows are to milk.
      This analogy relates an animal to the product created by that animal.
   Notes are to music as letters are to words.
      This analogy relates a part of something to the whole created by the parts.

4. Answers will vary.
   seconds : minutes :: minutes : hours
      There are 60 seconds in a minute. There are 60 minutes in an hour.
   days : weeks :: months : years
      Days are parts of a week. Months are parts of a year.
   October : fall :: January : winter
      October is a month in fall. January is a month in winter.
   Flag Day : June :: Mother's Day : May
      Flag Day is a June holiday. Mother's Day is a May holiday.

6. Answers will vary.
   Dog is to *bark* as *cat* is to *meow.*
      The relationship is an animal matched to the sound it makes. *Soft* isn't a sound made by a cat. *Meow* is a sound made by a cat.
   Inches are to feet as cents are to dollars.
      The relationship is a part to a whole. Inches are parts of a foot. Cents are not parts of miles. Cents are parts of dollars.
   Sweet is to *sour* as *soft* is to *hard.*
      This analogy starts with opposites. Sweet is the opposite of sour, but soft is not the opposite of gentle. Hard is the opposite of soft.

7. Answers will vary.
   candle : lantern :: lightbulb : lamp
      A candle can create the light in a lantern, while a lightbulb can create the light in a lamp.
   ink : pen :: paint : paintbrush
      Ink is the fluid that comes from a pen. Paint is the fluid that comes from a paintbrush.
   burner : oven :: faucet : sink
      A burner is part of an oven. A faucet is part of a sink.

8. Answers will vary.

9. Answers will vary.
   Angry is to *yell* as *happy* is to laugh.
      Angry people sometimes yell, and happy people sometimes laugh.
   Ice skater is to *rink* as *runner* is to track.
      Skaters perform in skating rinks or ice rinks. Runners perform on tracks or roads.
   Pear is to *fruit* as *celery* is to *vegetable.*
      A pear is a fruit. Celery is a vegetable.
   Gasoline is to *car* as *electricity* is to television.
      Gasoline powers cars. Electricity powers televisions.

Page 44
1. writer
2. kilometer
3. egg
4. bird
5. reptile
6. chirp
7. hour
8. jacket
9. percussion
10. brisk
11. slowly
12. sink

Page 45
Answers for 4, 6, and 7 will vary.
1. Jessica Dickensen left for Walt Disney World last Tuesday, March 17.
   My grandmother taught me to play cribbage on the plane ride to Florida.
   I loved visiting Universal Studios but had the most fun swimming at Daytona Beach.
2. Friday   Washington
   January   Pennsylvania Avenue
   government   freedom
   Jefferson Memorial   United States
3. Fables and What They Mean
   The Mystery of Timber Ridge
   A Guide to Making Quilts
   The Art of Making Tackles
8. Tessier and Sons, Inc.
   42 Pine Crest Lane
   Gingerville, MA 40511
9. Common Nouns   Proper Nouns
   motorcycle   Honda
   cell phone   Jacob
   monument   America
       Spanish
       Kansas
       Amazon
       Brazil
       Harriet
       Arbor Day

Page 46

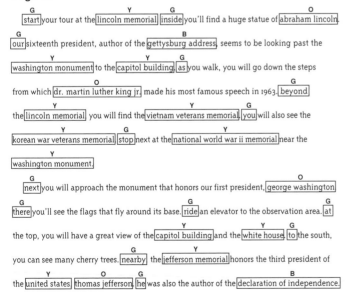

G — start your tour at the lincoln memorial Y — inside you'll find a huge statue of abraham lincoln. our sixteenth president, author of the gettysburg address, seems to be looking past the washington monument to the capitol building, as you walk, you will go down the steps from which dr. martin luther king jr. made his most famous speech in 1963. beyond the lincoln memorial you will find the vietnam veterans memorial, you will also see the korean war veterans memorial stop next at the national world war ii memorial near the washington monument.

next you will approach the monument that honors our first president, george washington there you'll see the flags that fly around its base. ride an elevator to the observation area. at the top, you will have a great view of the capitol building and the white house, to the south, you can see many cherry trees. nearby the jefferson memorial honors the third president of the united states, thomas jefferson, he was also the author of the declaration of independence.

Page 47
Answers for 3 and 7–9 will vary.
1. Gymnastics is a popular sport.
   Men compete in six events.
   Women compete in four events.
   Which gymnastic event is your favorite?

   Answers will vary.
   Is gymnastics a popular sport?
   How many events do men compete in?
   How many events do women compete in?
   My favorite gymnastic event is the balance beam.

2. Makayla leaps, turns, and flips on the balance beam. (declarative)
   Will you compete in the floor exercises? (interrogative)
   What is her best event so far? (interrogative)
   Wow, his performance on the rings was perfect! (exclamatory)

4. Gymnasts perform to the music of their choice.
   Why is it that only two gymnasts from each country may qualify?
   Are you sure the routine can't be longer than 90 seconds?
   He knows he must touch the pommel horse with only his hands.
   or
   He knows he must touch the pommel horse with his hands only.

6. Run-on: He held the pose four seconds but then he flipped and raised his hands and he smiled.
   She kept tumbling and leaping she danced with a smile down to the last second.
   Fragment: When we went home.
   Because uneven bars are her best event.
   Rewritten sentences will vary.

Page 48
1. F
2. C
3. R; Before Jenn took lessons, she couldn't even do a somersault. Soon she was rolling and flipping all over the gym.
4. F
5. R; She didn't win a medal. Jenn didn't do very well at all.
6. R; She didn't give up. Jenn worked harder instead.
7. C
8. F
9. C
10. C
Fragment repairs will vary.

Page 49
Answers for 4 and 6–9 will vary.
1. Strawberry farms are located across the state.
   Local farmers supply grocery stores and restaurants.
   A fresh cup of berries has only 60 calories.
   Strawberries are high in Vitamin C.
2. Dairy farmers make sure their cows are healthy.
   Most dairy cows can get food and water all day.
   Milking equipment gets cleaned often.
3. Some tractors harvest corn from the field.
   A baler compresses hay into bales.
   Farmers use tractors that plant seeds.

Page 50
1. Mr. Jessup, my neighbor, planted a crop of corn in his backyard.
2. My mother buys ears of corn by the dozen.
3. The yellow corn is delicious.
4. Dad eats corn on the cob with lots of butter on it.
5. Missy, my classmate, planted flower bulbs in her yard last fall.
6. You can find flower bulbs at garden centers in the late summer.
7. She showed us the most beautiful gladiolas from her garden.
8. Missy's fourth-grade teacher was delighted with the flowers Missy gave her.
9. All plants require sunlight, water, air, and nutrients from the soil.
10. Seed packet labels tell how old the seeds are.
11. Some gardeners transplant seedlings into their gardens.
12. Gardening takes time and patience.

Sentences will vary.

Page 51

1. Answers will vary.
   lion prowls, monkey climbs, python slithers, trout swims

2. Answers will vary.
   harps lull, drums beat, trumpets blare, xylophones ring

3. Answers will vary.
   Backhoes and bulldozers move dirt.
   Cars and trucks clog the highway.
   Trains and tractor trailers carry cargo.

4. Squirrels and birds live in the oak.
   Bats and moths are nocturnal.
   The willow and the maple drop their leaves.
   The goat and sheep graze on the hill.

6. A <u>cat</u> <u>licks</u> its fur.   *Cat* is a singular noun and needs a singular verb (*licks*).

   <u>Ferrets</u> <u>lick</u> their fur.   *Ferrets* is a plural noun and needs a plural verb (*lick*).

   <u>Kittens</u> and <u>cats</u> <u>lick</u> their fur.   *Kittens and cats* is a compound subject, which needs a plural verb (*lick*).

   A <u>dogwood</u> <u>sways</u> in the wind.   *Dogwood* is a singular noun and needs a singular verb (*sways*).

   <u>Pines</u> <u>sway</u> in the wind.   *Pines* is a plural noun and needs a plural verb (*sway*).

   <u>Maples</u> and <u>birches</u> <u>sway</u> in the wind.   *Maples and birches* is a compound subject, which needs a plural verb (*sway*).

7. <u>One</u> of those trees <u>is</u> dead.
   The <u>dog</u> with the fleas <u>is</u> gone.
   Our <u>ride</u> to the mountains <u>was</u> restful.
   <u>Songs</u> like that one <u>are</u> upbeat.

8. Answers will vary.

9. A crayon or pen works for this project.
   Her notebook or workbook is in the drawer.
   A banana or pear makes a good snack.
   His backpack or bookbag is in the locker.

Page 52

Answers will vary.
P   1. <u>Scent</u>, <u>sound</u>, and <u>body language</u> are
P   2. <u>Sand</u> and a <u>tumbleweed</u> are
P   3. <u>claws</u> shovel
S   4. <u>flock</u> glides
P   5. <u>Guards</u> beep
S   6. <u>army</u> marches
S   7. <u>guard</u> signals
S   8. <u>adult</u> babysits.
P   9. <u>Grooming</u> and <u>wrestling</u> are
S 10. <u>rain</u> splashes
S 11. <u>snake</u> slithers
P 12. <u>eagle</u> and <u>jackal</u> are
P 13. <u>scorpion</u> and <u>cricket</u> become
S 14. <u>mob</u> waits
P 15. <u>squirrels</u> and <u>mongooses</u> share
S 16. <u>meerkat</u> dives

Page 53

Answers for 2, 4, and 6–9 will vary.
1. <u>A simple sentence</u> <u>has a subject and a predicate</u>.
   <u>A compound sentence</u> <u>contains at least two simple sentences</u>.

3. <u>The Statue of Liberty</u> <u>holds a torch in her right hand</u>.
   <u>She</u> <u>grasps a tablet in her left hand</u>.

   <u>The Liberty Bell</u> <u>was rung at the first public reading of the Declaration of Independence</u>.
   <u>It</u> <u>cracked badly on Washington's Birthday in 1846</u>.

Page 54

1. S   6. C   11. C
2. S   7. C   12. C
3. C   8. S   13. C
4. S   9. C   14. C
5. S   10. S   15. C

Sentences will vary.

Page 55

Answers for 1, 3, and 9 will vary.
2. **Common**   **Proper**
   school   New York City
   aquarium   United States
   museum   Liberty Bell
   country   Statue of Liberty
   holiday   Sacagawea
   chocolate   Mars

4. beaches   dishes   catches
   loaves   mixes   foxes
   dresses   wolves   echoes
   brushes   buzzes   heroes

6. sheep   children oxen
   people   teeth   feet
   women   deer   geese
   mice   moose

7. Michael's drawing
   moon's glow
   grass's color
   Lisa's work
   hurricane's eye
   glass's rim

8. parents' jobs
   people's homes
   children's eyes
   boxes' labels
   pianos' keys
   chefs' recipes

Page 56

Order of answers will vary.

Common Nouns		Proper Nouns
inventor	people	Thomas Edison
president		Franklin Roosevelt
store		Macy's
city	places	Menlo Park
state		New Jersey
company	things	General Electric
book		The World Dictionary of Science

Page 58

1. is   6. was solved   11. sputtered
2. is   7. seemed   12. were dodging
3. will crack 8. began unraveling 13. led
4. ducked   9. were   14. can wear
5. was   10. lost   15. used

Linking Verbs
Sentence 1   is
Sentence 2   is
Sentence 5   was
Sentence 7   seemed
Sentence 9   were

Helping Verbs
Sentence 3   will crack
Sentence 6   was solved
Sentence 8   began unraveling
Sentence 12   were dodging
Sentence 14   can wear

Action Verbs
Sentence 4   ducked
Sentence 10   lost
Sentence 11   sputtered
Sentence 13   lead
Sentence 15   used

Page 59

Answers for 2 and 9 will vary.

1.
Past	Present	Future
voted	vote	will vote
discovered	discover	will discover
proclaimed	proclaim	will proclaim
encouraged	encourage	will encourage

3.
Past	Present	Future
stole	steal	will steal
took	take	will take
shrank	shrink	will shrink
flew	fly	will fly

4. Crystal jumped over the hurdle.
   Crystal will jump over the hurdle.
   Derrick searched for the keys.
   Derrick will search for the keys.
   Sarah listened to the story.
   Sarah will listen to the story.

6. Sentences will vary; brought, taught, caught, knew, threw, drew

7. drink, drank; know, knew; come, came; shake, shook; wear, wore

8. boast, will boast; interrupt, will interrupt; permit, will permit; sparkle, will sparkle; whistle, will whistle

Page 60

Past	Present			
✓		1. Yesterday, our class _____ on a field trip to Colonial Williamsburg.	P goes	Ⓞ went
	✓	2. Actors at Colonial Williamsburg _____ the part of colonial Americans daily.	Ⓗ play	K played
✓		3. Carpenters laid floors, framed walls, and _____ doors.	A hang	Ⓞ hung
	✓	4. On our next visit, we'll take photos that _____ workers laying shingles on the roof of a house.	Ⓘ show	U showed
✓		5. We _____ weavers work with wool, flax, and hemp for 30 minutes.	S watch	Ⓓ watched
	✓	6. Now, students, _____ that the brown wool is dyed using walnuts.	Ⓜ remember	T remembered
	✓	7. Shoemakers still _____ shoes in Colonial Williamsburg.	Ⓔ craft	R crafted
✓		8. In colonial days, presses _____ laws, record books, and a gazette.	V print	Ⓝ printed
	✓	9. Today printers at Colonial Williamsburg _____ books as colonial printers did.	Ⓞ bind	I bound
	✓	10. Blacksmiths today still _____ bars of iron until they become yellow.	Ⓓ heat	K heated
	✓	11. Some of us _____ our ears when the blacksmith hammers the metal.	Ⓣ cover	L covered
✓		12. Basketmakers _____ flexible ribbons of wood as we watched.	C weave	Ⓘ wove
✓		13. Yesterday we _____ how nimble your fingers had to be to make baskets.	B notice	Ⓝ noticed
✓		14. As we left, we _____ we would always remember the day we went back in time.	F know	Ⓛ knew

THE OLD DOMINION

Page 61

Answers for 2 and 8 will vary.

1. The bus stopped, but it pulled away quickly.
   Sam began to laugh, and he couldn't stop.
   The nurse winked, and then she vanished.
3. It sprinted behind the door.
   He limped to the bench.
   She left the check.
   They basked in the bright sun.
4. The culprit outran him or The culprit outran her.
   I'll introduce you to her.
   We are grateful to them.
   There wasn't much damage to it.
6. Sarah and I shoot baskets daily.
   Jay gave the books to Kim and me.
   April told Ala and me her plans.
   Tim and I love to skate.
7. We is always a subject.
9. Who cooked the turkey?
   Whom are you expecting?
   Whom should I ask?
   Who signed the declaration?

Page 62

1. The grounds crew mowed the field and used paint to mark it off.
2. Sara, a photographer, checks her backpack to be sure she has a rain tarp.
3. A cameraperson asks, "Is this your lens cover or mine?"
4. Members of the drill team roll up their flags and place them on the sidelines.
5. Mike, an announcer, tests his microphone by saying, "Test, test."
6. The American flag is raised to its proper height.
7. Some cheerleaders think they should try that cheer just one more time.
8. "We need some more towels over here," says one manager to another.
9. Jason, the mascot, thinks he should practice his victory dance.
10. "Don't make us laugh," begged the majorettes.
11. "Mom and I want two bags of popcorn," a boy says at the concession stand.
12. "If you ask me, we've never had a better team," said the coach.
13. Cheerleaders pull the giant banner tight so the players can burst through it.
14. In that moment, we're sure there's no team better than ours.

Page 63

Answers for 2–4 and 6–8 will vary.

1.
How	When	Where
slowly	annually	outside
gently	early	inside
swiftly		around
happily		high

9.
	Comparative	Superlative
hard	harder	hardest
early	earlier	earliest
well	better	best
badly	worse	worst

Page 67

1. Sentences will vary. Dependent clauses:
   Because she wanted to paint.
   Who eats in the cafeteria.
   When I see the doctor.

2. Dependent:
      when the coast is clear
      because he isn't feeling well
   Independent:
      She wore blue jeans.
      The chef made cupcakes.

3. We need more kindling because the fire went out. or Because the fire went out, we need more kindling.
   When the wolves howled, shivers went down my spine. or Shivers went down my spine when the wolves howled.
   It was your brother who prepared our dinner.

4. Sentences will vary.
   the broken CD player, a fluffy pillow, my favorite books, my sister's blanket, the empty mug

6. I should have helped them.
   She will be going home soon.
   It has been raining all day.
   We could have painted a picture.

7. The ball rolled under the bed. (where)
   The pen was in my desk. (where)
   On Saturday, the train will stop. (when)
   Let's stretch before the race. (when)

8. Ms. Pugh, my second-grade teacher, was there.
   Spencer College, the first one in this area, closed.
   Mr. Dennis, the mayor, will speak first.
   Aunt Lily, my dad's sister, came for a short visit.

9. Answers will vary.

Page 68

	dependent	independent
1. at home	M	(N)
2. in the day, before dark	(O)	S
3. near still water	P	(T)
4. of your campfire	E	(R)
5. at least 100 feet, from your tent	(A)	B
6. no prepositional phrase	K	(C)
7. no prepositional phrase	(E)	R
8. of twigs and rocks	B	(Y)
9. of anthills	(O)	T
10. no prepositional phrase	S	(U)
11. in each tent corner	(R)	A
12. on top, of sleeping pads	E	(V)
13. After dark	S	(I)
14. from a clean source	(S)	C
15. of all, of nature	W	(I)
16. with plenty, of water	(T)	Y

Leave <u>NO TRACE</u> of <u>YOUR VISIT</u>.

Page 69

Answers for 1 and 6–9 will vary.
2. When we go camping, I help Dad with the tent. Revised sentences will vary.
3. because, since, after, before, unless, while; Clauses and sentences will vary.
4. <u>After we went to the movies,</u> we stopped for pizza and ice cream.

Sentences will vary.

Page 70

Sentences will vary.

Part 1: Added clauses should be underlined in orange.
1. Although it was very late (red)
2. because I didn't feel well (red)
3. since we were out of school (red)
4. Before I leave for school (red)
5. Until I earn some money (red)
6. so that my parents will be proud (red)

Part 2: Added clauses should be underlined in red.
7. Mark's team won the game (orange)
8. I can't play today (orange)
9. my teacher always smiles (orange)
10. Mom said I could get a new camera (orange)
11. we'll need to wash the car (orange)
12. Our principal will be on television (orange)

Page 71

Answers for 2–4 and 6–9 will vary.
1. I went to school, gymnastics, and church.
   The list included potatoes, bananas, and yogurt.
   I need scissors, glue, and a notebook.
   She has red, yellow, orange, and blue yarn.

Page 72

1. All fish, ferrets, and gerbils are on sale this week.
2. Because so many dogs need homes, we also feature pups from shelters.
3. Our basic grooming package includes bathing, clipping, and nail trimming.
4. We have adoption fairs every Sunday at our store in Sacramento, California.
5. Zachary, could you show this gentleman where we keep the betta food?
6. We only sell geckos at our location in Richmond, Virginia.
7. I thought the guinea pig cages had already been cleaned, Burt.
8. Even though all puppies are adorable, not all of them make good pets for small apartments.
9. Pepper, the older black schnauzer, is ready for his red bandana.
10. Our "Positively Purr-fect" sale begins Saturday, February 10, at 9:00 AM.
11. Wow, we are overstocked on cat food.
12. Matt whispered, "Be gentle" as he passed the rabbit to the boy.
13. Ferrets are due to arrive by Tuesday, September 10.
14. Oh my, the chameleon is on the loose again.
15. Someone heard the cockatiel shout, "Atta boy!"
16. Koi, a type of Japanese fish, make excellent pets for garden ponds.

Page 72 (continued)

items in a series
   1, 3
a city and state
   4, 6
a dependent clause from an independent clause that follows it
   2, 8
the name of a person spoken to
   5, 7

in dates
   10, 13
to set off an interjection
   11, 14
to set off spoken words
   12, 15
to set off a phrase that explains
   9, 16

Page 73

Answers for 2–4 and 6–9 will vary.
1. "You have practice this Saturday," Mom said.
   "Hey, guys!" Peter yelled. "Look at that airplane."

Page 74

1. Crowds chanted, "<u>Let us in!</u>" as they waited for the doors to open.
2. Then someone shouted, "<u>There's a limo headed this way</u>!"
3. "<u>Step back</u>," the usher said. "<u>Please remain behind the velvet ropes.</u>"
4. A chauffeur opened the door and warned, "<u>Watch your step, sir.</u>"
5. Heartthrob Harry emerged saying, "<u>Would you look at this crowd</u>?"
6. He whispered, "<u>Where did all these people come from, dude</u>?"
7. "<u>How's my hair</u>?" he asked as he checked his reflection.
8. "<u>Check to see if I have some spinach in my teeth, please</u>," he begged.
9. "<u>Oh, look!</u>" a young girl shouted. "<u>There's Babette!</u>"
10. As cameras clicked, Babette smiled and asked, "<u>How's this</u>?"
11. "<u>Isn't this dress divine</u>?" the diva crooned.
12. She admitted, "<u>It was designed by Sara Chang.</u>"
13. Then she revealed her new pocket pooch, saying, "<u>Isn't it the cutest thing</u>?"
14. Girls lining the red carpet chimed, "<u>Awwww!</u>"
15. A bodyguard motioned for the couple to move on, saying, "<u>It's almost showtime.</u>"
16. Whisking Babette inside, Harry shouted to the crowd, "<u>You're going to love the show!</u>"

Page 75

Answers for 2–4 and 6–9 will vary.
1. Yesterday, I had the best day ever! During morning announcements, I was named Citizen of the Week. Then the cafeteria served my favorite lunch. In my last class, science, I got an A on my test. If only every day could be that great.

Page 77

Answers for 2–9 will vary.
1. "You have practice this Saturday," Mom said.
   "Hey guys," Peter yelled, "Look at that plane!"
   As he scratched his head, Jake mumbled, "I'm not sure."

Page 83

Answers for 1, 3–4, and 6–9 will vary.
2.

Friendly Letter	Both	Business Letter
heading starts at center	heading: sender's address and date	heading starts at left
no inside address		has an inside address
greeting ends with a comma	greeting says Dear [Name]	greeting ends with a colon
body has indented paragraphs	body	body is not indented
closing starts at center	first letter of closing is a capital followed by a comma	closing starts at left
signature is handwritten and starts at center	signature is handwritten	signature is handwritten and typed and starts at left

Page 86

1. g
2. m
3. d
4. e
5. h
6. j
7. k
8. a
9. l
10. f
11. b
12. n
13. i
14. c

Page 88

1. A
2. T
3. D
4. A
5. T
6. E
7. T
8. D
9. T
10. D
11. E
12. A
13. A
14. D
15. D
16. E
17. D
18. E